T0087606

Exercises in the Elements

Josef Pieper Books Published by St. Augustine's Press

Exercises in the Elements

Essays – Speeches – Notes

Josef Pieper

ST. AUGUSTINE'S PRESS

South Bend, Indiana

Manufactured in the United States of America.

1 2 3 4 5 6   25 24 23 22 21 20 19

Library of Congress Cataloging in Publication Data

Names: Pieper, Josef, 1904-1997, author.
Farrelly, Daniel J., 1934-
translator.
Title: Exercises in the elements: essays, speeches, notes / Josef Pieper ;
translation by Dan Farrelly.
Description: South Bend, Indiana: St. Augustine's Press, Inc., 2016.
Includes bibliographical references and index.
Identifiers: LCCN 2016035079
ISBN 9781587312311 (cloth : alk. paper)
ISBN 9781587312328 (paperbound : alk. paper)
Subjects: LCSH: Philosophy.
Philosophical theology.
Classification: LCC B3323.P432 E5 2016
DDC 193--dc23 LC record available at https://lccn.loc.gov/2016035079

St. Augustine's Press
www.staugustine.net

"Spelling is not yet reading; but it does lead to it."
Goethe
(To Riemer, 6. II. 1806)

Contents

Preface

In giving this book the title "Exercises in the Elements" [Buch-stabier-Übungen] the author of the attempts at clarification summarized here had two guide-lines in mind which perhaps seem strangely at variance with one another. The first was the prolog to the *Summa Theologiae* of Thomas Aquinas, and the second a text from Bertolt Brecht.

Anyone who did not know how little the last of the great teachers of the as yet undivided Christendom was inclined to irony could see it as a well-aimed polemical understatement when Thomas says of his *opus magnum* that it is not for "advanced" readers but "for the instruction of beginners."

I had this excellent declaration of his intention in mind. And of course, as I am well aware, the possibilities of finding an analogy to that fundamental book reflecting the European tradition of wisdom are already exhausted.

Far less embarrassing is the thought of a different kind of model: namely, the relatively well-known Brecht poem which formulates a series of aggressive "questions of a reading worker." What to me appeared important in this was not its socially critical orientation but the unswerving insistence on an answer which does not cheat us of things which are elementary and obvious.

This is exactly the aim of the following exercises: that precisely this elementary aspect—which in learned writings is all too often and without much thought "presupposed" and therefore left out—be identified and named as clearly as possible, almost as in a primer or catechism, so that it remains unforgotten.

What Does Interpretation Mean?

The most precise answer I have seen for a long time is that of the Canadian theologian Bernard Lonergan.[1] He says: "An Interpretation is the expression of the meaning of another expression." As one can see, a formulation with the deceptive simplicity characteristic of a phrase that hits the bullseye. The first problem arises when one tries to translate this definition (into German)—in other words, to interpret it. (Translation is indeed a fundamental form of interpretation, and, in a certain sense, all interpretation can be understood as translation.) The problem in this present case is that the word "expression," used twice, does not have the same meaning each time. The first time it means an activity, giving expression to something; whereas in the second case it is a substantive: something expressed. Interpreting means giving expression to what is meant by something already said by someone else.

The one who interprets is dealing with a particular kind of utterance: namely, with an utterance by which the person expressing himself means something. In short, he is dealing with an utterance that is meaningful—or, more accurately—significant. This comes about when, and only when, an intellectually gifted person actively, through perceptible signs, points to something different from these signs themselves and makes others aware of it. Amongst those perceptible signs a prominent place is occupied, undoubtedly, by the word, whether spoken or written. But also a bodily gesture—a shake of the head, for example, or a hand held out in greeting—

1   Bernard J. F. Lonergan, *Insight*. London 1957, p. 586.

belongs equally to the sphere of significant utterances, like all human symbolic activity. When Christopher Columbus came to Cuba and found in the natives' settlements a blade of grass placed before the door, as much as to say "entry not wanted," he saw himself confronted by an obviously significant utterance which he had to interpret to find its meaning—interpret in the strict sense. And, of course, musical or visual works of art are likewise deliberately constructed significant utterances.

Moreover, the deliberate nature of the communication does not necessarily imply that it would have happened consciously. An unconscious smile or furrowing of the brow is also a positive act which points to something else. Even in a spoken utterance, the use of a particular word can be intended to mean something of which the speaker is not conscious—something which possibly becomes clear to him only when he feels he is misunderstood. Perhaps we are not at all able to be fully conscious of what every word we use daily really means—even of what we ourselves subjectively mean by it.

That "something" which is different from the signs and which is pointed to by a significant utterance cannot well be understood as anything that is not in some way real; an utterance is significant and therefore able to be interpreted precisely because it points to reality. If, for example, someone states that the sentence "The world is created" is not a significant utterance but rather a meaningless statement, what he means by this is that there is no reality to which this sentence can refer and that, accordingly, the sentence is neither capable of or in need of interpretation.

On the basis of the above, with regard to the *object*, the concept of interpretation in the strict sense can be distinguished with some clarity from both a too broad and a too narrow usage. Of course, both types of usage are encountered in common speech. That the concept "interpretation" is used in too narrow a sense is obvious enough where it is limited—as in the case of both

Schleiermacher[2] and Dilthey[3]—to spoken or written utterance (or "text"). Much more difficult is the distinction from various broader meanings of the concept—as, for example, when Bacon[4] or Galileo speak of an "interpretation of nature," or when the Festschrift[5] for Guardini has the title "Interpretation of the World." And is it not possible to speak justifiably of the interpretation of a neurotic symptom? But, above all, what are we to make of the "classical" case of interpretation of dreams, where the term is used not only in psychoanalysis[6] but also in the Bible. It is used more than twenty times just in the Vulgate translation of the Book of Daniel alone. My answer to this is that, in the instances mentioned, we can in fact speak of "interpretation" in the strict sense—*under certain presuppositions.* As long as research into nature sees itself, no matter how vaguely and noncommittally, as "a reading in the book of nature"—and therefore as interpretation of a text by which the author has meant something—and as long as the things which derive from the divine Logos as *creatura* have themselves the "character of word" according to Guardini's formulation,[7] the quality of interpretability can be attributed to nature and to the world as a whole. Of course, it has to be kept in mind *who*, in fact, ought to be the interpreter of that which is

2   Fr. Schleiermacher, *Hermeneutik*. Edited by H. Kimmerle. Heidelberg 1959, p. 124.

3   *Die Entstehung der Hermeneutik. Gesammelte Schriften V*, 1. 4th edition Stuttgart/Göttingen 1964, p. 317. See also W.Babilas, Tradition und Interpretation. Munich 1961, p. 37.

4   "Interpretation of Nature"—a phrase used by Bacon to denote the discovery of natural laws by means of induction. Oxford Dictionary. Article Interpretation.

5   Würzburg 1965.

6   P. Ricoeur, *Die Interpretation. Ein Versuch über Freud*. Frankfurt 1969, p. 39.

7   *Welt und Person*. Würzburg 1940, p. 110.

interpretable. Furthermore, individual occurrences in nature, such as storms, the flight of birds, the flow of sacrificial blood, can rightly be seen as interpretable perhaps only by those who are interpreters by calling and have some legitimation—as long as all of these occurrences are considered a communication by some supra-human spiritual power. And possibly even the neurotic symptom is likewise understandable and interpretable in the strict sense insofar as the psychotherapist can take it to be an utterance of one who "basically knows his own mind."[8] But as far as the dreams are concerned, the attempt to interpret them can mean two things: both a causal "explanation" (based on the interaction, let us say, between libido, need for admiration, early childhood experiences, etc.) and an interpretation which precisely does *not* "explain" but is to be understood as the task of a prophetic mind interpreting a divine message. In the biblical context, interpretation of dreams has only this latter meaning.

To sum up: giving a valid interpretation of a significant utterance means to understand its author's meaning and to mediate it, i.e., make it comprehensible to others. But this is a highly ambitious undertaking.

The first and crucial element of the concept, the understanding of what is meant by the significant utterance, can only be achieved on the supposition that a multiplicity of only imperfectly fulfillable demands are met which, into the bargain, cannot even be adequately named. Schleiermacher formulated one of the most important demands in his brief statement: "All understanding of the individual thing is dependent on understanding the whole."[9] But how much is included in this "whole"? —To begin with, a significant utterance is naturally part of a broader thought context.

---

8   A. Görres, *Methode und Erfahrung der Psychoanalyse*. Munich 1958, p. 274.

9   *Hermeneutik*, p. 467; also p. 141.

And it is almost a cliché, although a completely apt one, to say that if we are not to misinterpret a statement we are "not to take it out of context." But in fact this is what happens all the time, not just in journalistic debate concerning current politics—which lives by such methods—but also in literature which has a claim to being scientific. An absolutely unbelievable example of this is to be found in the "History of Logic in the Western World" by Carl Prantl (Geschichte der Logik im Abendland), published[10] one hundred years ago in several volumes and reprinted in a new unchanged edition in 1955 by the Wissenschaftliche Buchgesellschaft Darmstadt. It is still seen as the standard work and, for example, in the short "History of Logic" (Geschichte der Logik) by Heinrich Scholz is praised[11] precisely for its "admirable mastery of the material"[12] and its "exemplary exactitude in its presentation of the source material." The truth is that precisely these qualities are the ones which are definitely missing from Prantl's work. For example, the author has hardly understood anything of the logic of Aquinas which he discusses at length in his book—not only because he takes individual sentences "out of their context," but also because he bases his judgments and condemnations on statements which, while they are indeed to be found in the *Summa theologiae*, are there as "Objektionen," i.e., as formulations of views which Thomas himself refutes. The "whole" which Prantl should have understood from the beginning, if he was to understand and correctly interpret the statements he quotes, was no more than the structure of the scholastic *articulus*—on average, one page in length. An historian could be expected to read the *articulus* in its entirety.

But, of course, a significant utterance is not feasible except in

10   Leipzig 1855–1870; second edition 1927.
11   Berlin 1931, p. v.
12   An exception is J. M. Bocheński, who says: "It is better totally to ignore him (Prantl)" (*Formale Logik*. Freiburg/Munich 1956, p. 10).

a language context. And only someone who "has a command" of the language spoken in a particular historical region at a particular time is at all equipped to understand something concretely expressed in it. It begins with the knowledge of vocabulary and grammar—and this is a precondition which is much more seldom met than people generally think. Socrates' statement, for example, that he does not know, of himself, why a person is not allowed to take his own life but rather that he knows it *ex akoés,*[13] *ex auditu* (as Marsilio Ficino says in his Plato translation; and the Vulgate translates the same phrase occurring in the Epistle to the Romans (10, 17)—that faith comes *ex akoés,* i.e., from hearing)—this, as you would think, completely clear statement of Socrates is rendered in all the German translations I know (Schleiermacher, Apelt, Rufener) of Plato's "Phaedo" dialog: "from hearsay"!

Moreover, it is obvious here that the interpreter must not only know and have a command of the "foreign language" from which the utterance is to be translated but must likewise have a command of his own language in which he expresses his interpretation and communicates it—again something which cannot be taken for granted. If someone with responsibility for the official new German version of the Bible seriously thinks that the word "beatitude" (Seligkeit) means in current everyday German "a condition enjoyed by children, lovers, drunks and also the dead,"[14] so that the "beatitudes" of the Sermon on the Mount no longer make sense—then it is permitted to ask whether anyone who is so little at home in his own language is not thereby disqualified as a translator and interpreter.

But someone who wants to be able to understand and properly interpret a concrete significant utterance must know much more than the peculiarities of the language of a particular country. In every

13   *Phaedo* 61 d.
14   *Gottesdienst.* 6 (1972), p. 153.

historical language we can think of there is an infinity of modalities for expressing the same thought, and they, too, are an essential component of that "whole" that is always going to be misunderstood. I am thinking, for example, of the famous sentence from the final chapter of St. Augustine's "Confessions": "We see things because they are; but they are because You see them";[15] and I ask myself whether what is meant here can be completely grasped by someone who did not understand that this hymnic prayer says exactly the same as the conceptually sober sentence of Thomas Aquinas, according to which the things we find in world, by their very nature, "exist between two knowing faculties"—the divine and the human.[16]

Furthermore, for a person who does not already have direct knowledge of the fact that literature, along with factual statement, is an essential part of the "whole" of our forms of expression, and who does not understand the "point" of it, whole provinces of what can be said in human language must inevitably remain closed to him—and not just the province, in the narrower sense, of literature. Thus we might wonder what a learned translator and commentator could understand and make intelligible to others about the meaning of the Canticle of Canticles if he suspects that it "originally" was "an invitation to join a spiritual society."[17] Naturally, someone who is capable of valid interpretation must also know that there is such a thing as irony and must be able to recognize it. And how can an over-serious, perhaps foreign interpreter who does not suspect that there is such a thing as a playful use of language understand and make others understand a "Gallows Song" of Christian Morgenstern ("Jaguar, Zebra, Mink, Mandrill ..."—how much must one be aware of if one is not to be completely lost when

15 *Confessions* 13, 38.
16 *Quaest.disp. de Veritate* I, 2. Gottesdienst
17 Riessler/Storr, *Die Heilige Schrift des Alten und des Neuen Bundes*. 10th impression Mainz 1959, p. 1358.

confronted with verse like this!). It is also obvious that one must be prepared for the possibility of the sophist's misuse of language, the political speak, the propaganda, the almost completely ubiquitous presence of commercial advertising, where what is said has no meaning except to achieve an aim ("The Stuyvesant Generation is going its own way"), etc. The possibilities are legion.

In summary: the practitioner who specializes in *a* form of human expression, or even in one sole form, no matter how important the text (and the literature about this text) is clearly *not* equipped for accurate interpretation, perhaps not even of that exclusively studied text. To achieve valid interpretation one would really need, from one's own experience, to know all forms of human communication, within the totality of which a concrete utterance may be understood to be situated. "One would really need"—this points to the crucial question which has almost been answered already: whether an interpretation, provided we are considering, above all, the great subjects that are worthy of our efforts to understand and render them understandable, is not by its very nature an unending task.

But now we have to deal expressly with something which until now, although it belongs to the preconditions of understanding, has not formally been addressed. A significant utterance, the sole object of interpretation in the strict sense, is essentially concerned, as we have said, with reality. The interpreter must focus principally on this reference to reality. He must try to grasp it. We can say: he must consider the claim to truth made by the utterance. (Truth is, after all, the same as reality coming into view!) To put it plainly: the interpreter must really "listen to" the utterance and to the one who makes the utterance. Perhaps that seems very obvious. However, the reality is that in the average case of dealing with important philosophical and literary utterances from the past what happens is the opposite of "listening." The utterances are received very attentively, but *without* the references to reality that they contain, i.e., without consideration of what the author primarily meant—without really listening to him.

There is still something that needs to be said about this *not*-listening in dealing with an utterance. During World War II I was working as an "Armed Forces Psychologist." In the assessment of future officers, pilots, and specialists the "examinee" was required first to give a brief description of his circumstances (family, education, favorite subjects, hobbies, etc.). One of the assessors led the conversation while all the others listened carefully and diligently took notes. The young narrator probably became more and more convinced that what he was saying was arousing a quite unusual degree of interest. But if he had been able to see what the psychologists were writing down, for instance about the lively or stiff expression on his face, his easy or tense attitude, the way he spoke his vowels or consonants, he would then quite rightly have said: You are not listening to me! He would have been disappointed and would have felt insulted. Everyone expects and takes for granted that he is listened to when he speaks, i.e., that the other person does not primarily focus on the peculiarities of his form of utterance or the source of his images and vocabulary. He is also not content that the other person is satisfied not to hear anything more than what he, the speaker, thinks. As a rule, he is not simply looking for approval. He naturally wants his utterance to be considered, i.e., to be judged as to whether it is true or false, appropriate, enlightening, fruitful, etc. —All of this applies equally when we are dealing with authors like Plato or Thomas Aquinas.

Whatever about all scholarly study of source material, only the person who listens to his author is in a position to interpret him. To quote Rudolf Bultmann:[18] "Interpretation always presupposes a living rapport to the things" being dealt with.

18 Das Problem der Hermeneutik. *Zeitschrift für Theologie und Kirche*, 47 (1950), p. 54; p. 62.

It should be clear that with this preliminary formulation the relationship between interpretation and history is up for discussion—an extremely difficult, sensitive issue about which I would like to make some comments, though more in the nature of aphorisms than systematically.

Of course, it must be said straightaway that interpreting something which is not directly present is not feasible without history. But that does not mean that we are dealing with a proportion of such a kind that a plus on one side would *eo ipso* increase the possibilities on the other side. There are important examples of brilliant interpretation where historical knowledge is very limited and even despite individual notions which are historically completely false. Thus it seems to me a highly significant fact that an Aristotle commentary which up to the present has not been surpassed was written by a man who had very little knowledge of Greek and knew nothing about the genesis of this book which he considered to be deliberately planned as a systematic book and as a completely rounded whole, whereas historical research has meanwhile shown us that it is a chance collection of very different texts. This man is Thomas Aquinas. Of course, it could be said that he could have made a much better commentary if he had been able to base his work—instead of on the rough and ready, but adequate Latin translation—on the Oxford critical edition of Sir David Ross. But we must still consider that it is not impossible truly to listen to a voice which we hear imperfectly; and this listening, primarily directed to the reality reference of what is said—to the author's meaning— can result in a penetrating exploration, not only of the text itself but also of the substance of what it says, to an extent that has hardly ever been achieved despite the increased perfection of historical and philological text criticism. But the problematic nature of the relationship between interpretation and history goes deeper. This becomes apparent above all when we consider that tradition— by which we mean retaining in translation the identical meaning of something said as it is handed on into the language of the present— can only happen through valid interpretation. The relationship between history and interpretation is to be seen as analogous to that between history and tradition. But just as, according to Theodor Schieder,[19] the paradox in "historical thinking" lies in the fact that, "on the one hand it preserves the memory and on the other hand dissolves it" and that it "on the one hand wants to pass it on but on the other hand threatens to destroy it," so, too, can the historical way of seeing things inhibit an interpretation in the strict sense or even prevent it—interpretation understood as inquiry into what is meant by the utterance: its reference to reality, and that means its truth (or otherwise).

Of course, it is now time to correct and define more precisely the already mentioned preliminary formulation "History and Interpretation." The "historical way of thinking," the "historical thinking" of which Theodor Schieder speaks (in the same context he also uses the word "Historicism")—all of this, although it perhaps signals, so to speak, a danger inherent in the historian's profession, is naturally something quite different from history itself. On the other hand, it remains true that anyone who looks at significant utterances—which he finds in the history of human thought—purely under their "historical aspect" is by the same token incapable of genuine interpretation. In this point it must be conceded that Mephisto—introduced into literature by C. S. Lewis as *Screwtape*—because of the extent of his practical experience was right. The *Screwtape Letters*, first published in London in 1942, is a superb, both witty and profound as well as serious back-to-front anthropology (published in the English-speaking world in innumerable editions and familiar to every educated person, but available to us only in a mediocre translation as "Instructions for

---

19   See J. Pieper, *Über den Begriff der Tradition*. Cologne-Opladen 1958, p. 43.

a lower class of devil" (Dienstanweisung an einen Unterteufel[20]). This *opusculum* is comprised of pieces of advice which Mr. Screwtape gives a beginner who is not yet advanced in the art of leading people astray. And when the pupil, sincerely worried, mentions the fact that very intelligent people read the books of wisdom of the ancients, his teacher reassures him with the comment: "the historical point of view," to which scholars in the Western world have been brought by the devilish spirits, means precisely that the only question that will certainly never be asked will be the question about the truth of what has been read. Instead of that, people ask about influences and dependencies, the development of the writer in question, the influence he has exerted, etc.[21] It is no less important, I think, to keep in mind the contemporary fact of which I have just now received further confirmation from reliable experts that in countries under communist rule, where editions of works in the "Western" tradition are readily available (for instance, of Plato or Dante), these works are accompanied by an introduction which supplies the reader with an "historical" understanding of the author which openly aims (although hopefully not always with success) at preventing the reader from taking what he reads too seriously. Naturally, these explanations might not amount to proper history. However, it seems to me that what they actually say is less important than the deliberate distraction, which focuses the reader's attention not on the substance of the work itself and its reference to reality but on the author and on the elements which condition his communication; the crucial point is, in other words, to prevent the kind of listening which is the precondition of understanding and interpretation.

Anyone who attempts to investigate what is meant by a

---

20 Freiburg (Herder-Bücherei no.545). 18th impression 1978.
21 *The Screwtape Letters*. Fontana Books. 15th impression. London 1965, pp. 139f.

significant utterance is clearly never dealing *exclusively* with this, in one way or another, objectified utterance—with a text, for example—but necessarily also with the someone who makes the utterance. He is the one who, by uttering, means something, i.e., wants to communicate and make something knowable. There is also, on the basis of the nature[22] peculiar to all beings who have the gift of mind, a communality embracing the person interpreted and the person interpreting, without which, indeed, understanding and interpreting would not be possible[23]—so that it has rightly been declared unthinkable that there could be a significant utterance which is completely closed to all possibility of comprehension. But an interpretation that is not just roughly accurate but gets to the heart of the utterance will only come about where there is a personal affinity which goes beyond the shared spirit-nature. I am referring to that *connaturalitas* by virtue of which a direct grasp of the ultimate meaning is possible which far surpasses in accuracy all logical argumentation, so that the other is seen almost as one's own. Affinity of this kind is spoken about again and again in all theory of interpretation. Dilthey speaks of the necessity of "an affinity, heightened by intensive sharing of life with the author."[24] Here perhaps the "divinatory" element comes into play which Schleiermacher[25] sees as an intuitive "female" force alongside what he calls the "comparative" rational male element at work in every interpretation. This force alone is capable, with unerring instinct, to divine that which is also unsaid[26] by an author because he takes it for granted.

22 Fr. Ast, *Grundlinien der Grammatik, Hermeneutik und Kritik. Landshut* 1808, p. 172.
23 O. Fr. Bollnow, *Das Verstehen.* Mainz 1949, p. 29.
24 *Die Entstehung der Hermeneutik*, pp. 329f.
25 *Hermeneutik*, p. 109.
26 See M. Heidegger, *Platons Lehre von der Wahrheit.* Bern 1947, p. 5.

But in conclusion something must be said of the situation where one is confronted with the interpretation of an utterance, the author of which not only simply cannot be found or identified but even does not seem to be identically "one." Admittedly, that sounds mysterious, but a concrete example should make it clear. I quote here a passage from a posthumously published volume of essays by the actor Ernst Ginsberg[27] who speaks of a strange encounter. "Early one rainy morning in Zurich our doorbell rang at about 6 o'clock. When I opened the door, there stood Else Lasker-Schüler, visibly excited and distracted, her wet hair hanging down around her face. She apologized for her early visit and asked if she could read me a poem that had come to her during the night. Drenched as she was, she sat down on the couch in her coat and tiger-skin hat and read me the poem 'Die Verscheuchte'[28] ... Then she asked me abruptly: 'How do you find it?' I said how moved I was but she interrupted me quickly: 'No, no, not whether you like it, but'—and she pointed to a particular line: 'What does that there mean?' Assuming that the poet wanted only reassurance about the clarity of her words, I explained what I thought was the meaning of this passage. She stared at me wide-eyed and said in astonishment, in the singing intonation of her Elberfeld dialect: 'Yes, lad, it could have meant that!" —On the one hand, it is completely clear that those lines were written only by Else Lasker-Schüler in her own handwriting; on the other hand, it cannot be denied that she is not the only one, and perhaps she is not at all the one, who meant something particular by this utterance. But then, who would it be? Else Lasker-Schüler, hailed by so sober a critic as Bertolt Brecht

---

27   "Abschied." *Erinnerungen, Theateraufsätze. Gedichte*. Zurich 1965, pp. 154f.

28   Else Lasker-Schüler, *Gedichte 1902–1943*. Edited by Friedhelm Kemp, Munich 1959, p. 347.

as "a great poet,"[29] says of herself: "Writing takes place in me
... The writer does not intend anything; the more devoutly he
listens to his angel the more profound is his writing. People call
this condition: inspiration."[30]

These words of Else Lasker-Schüler are, although she probably did not know it, part of a long and great tradition. It stretches
from Plato[31]—who says of poets that they speak "in divine madness," in a frame of mind, at least, which is more out of itself than
present to itself—down to Goethe, who says the poet is "truly
bereft of his senses."[32]

In Christianity, the concept "inspiration" has taken on a
mainly *theological* meaning. By contrast to what we might call
"artistic" inspiration it is, on the one hand, more precisely definable, namely as divine authorship, working through a human
writer, of a text which for this very reason is called "holy"; on the
other hand, it reaches far more deeply down into regions on which
the ratio can shed no light.

Of course, it lies beyond the scope of the subject being discussed here, and also beyond my competence, to deal more in detail
with the theological concept of inspiration. The only important
question for us here is about the changed conditions for valid interpretation that this brings with it. To put it differently: it is a
question of the inner structure of theology—insofar as one understands by theology the attempt to interpret those "holy" texts, i.e.,
to hear, to understand, and to make comprehensible through the
medium of a human author the true meaning of what is truly
meant by the divine author. It is evident what acute need there is

29 Ginsberg, "Abschied", p. 153.
30 Ibid.
31 *Phaedrus*, 245 a.
32 F. W. Riemer, *Mitteilungen über Goethe*. Edited by Arthur Pollmer.
    Leipzig 1921, p. 334.

here for a valid interpretation—demands which one could almost say have become virtually impossible to meet.

I shall try to indicate how acute this need is, and how it might be met, by using two concrete examples.

The first example: the eschatological myths related by Plato's Socrates about the Last Judgement which awaits every human being and, in an unerring sentence, metes out reward and punishment. — Perhaps with some surprise one might ask how this can be seen as an example of interpretation of an "inspired" text. I would like to offer some thoughts about this. First, as all the Platonic dialogs clearly testify, neither Socrates nor Plato lay any claim to authorship of the myths they relate. It is always a question of *reporting* something that is already there. I consider that the view normally accepted in Plato literature that Plato the "myth maker" invented and wrote these stories himself[33]—as a product of his own original creative mind and with a view to giving his own ideas a more penetrating profile—can be proven to be false.[34] Furthermore, in his seventh letter Plato ascribes precisely the teaching about the Last Things to those "old and holy discourses," *tois palaiois te kai hierois logois*, which it is in fact, *óntos*, proper to believe.[35] The ones who express themselves in discourses of this kind are, in Plato's view, "the ancients,"[36] by which he does not mean "the aged," not the men with snow-white hair, but those "who live close to the gods,"[37] those who were the first to know[38] and receive and then communicate the knowledge brought

33 O. Apelt's translation of the word *mythos* (*Phaedo* 114 d 7) as "creative description" (*Philosoph. Bibliothek*, vol. 147, p. 128) is typical.
34 See J. Pieper, *Über die platonischen Mythen*. Munich 1965, p. 25; pp. 86f.
35 335 a 2–4.
36 See J. Pieper, *Überlieferung. Begriff und Anspruch*. Munich 1970, pp. 45ff.
37 *Philebos* 16 c 5–9.
38 *Phaedrus* 274 c I.

down from a divine source by an unknown Prometheus.[39] I can offer nothing that would distinguish conceptually the "ancients," who for Plato remain anonymous, from what Christian theology means by an "inspired" author (prophets, hagiographers).

The most immediate response of Plato's Socrates—an otherwise not easily convinced rational debater—faced with such sacred tradition authenticated by the "ancients" is: to accept it devoutly as truth. "You think it is only a story, but I think it is truth. And the reason I relate it to you is that it is true."[40] But this Socratic faith, with the strength of its assertion which throughout the ages links the believer in a community[41] with the "ancients" and above all with the supra-human power which speaks through it and which (as Karl Jaspers also does, with the necessary vagueness[42]) one could call a *corpus mysticum*—this faith creates and begets that affinity which is likewise here the crucial presupposition for understanding what is really meant and therefore also for valid interpretation. It is theology in the strict sense when Plato, interpreting, penetrates through the imagery of the judgment made at the crossroads in the field in the underworld to see what it really means: namely, that the ultimate manifestation of the true outcome of our existence in this world is made on the other side of death—in precisely this event which is something beyond our comprehension and experience and which in symbolic speech is called "Last Judgement." It is to be expected, and it is quite inevitable, that in his work of interpretation Plato uses the contemporary notions of the structure of the earth and the water channels running under its surface. Even a modern theologian, when he seriously undertakes to interpret some element of tradition as

39 *Philebos* 16 c 5–9.
40 *Gorgias* 523 a.
41 See J. Pieper, *Über den Glauben*. Munich 1962, pp. 45f.
42 *Philosophie*. 2ⁿᵈ impression. Berlin/Göttingen/Heidelberg 1948, p. 259.

truth, cannot simply neglect contemporary knowledge of the world and of man. The only thing that matters is that, despite all the historical conditioning elements, the supra-empirical divine message which only the person of faith can hear should, in its purity, be made present to the consciousness and retained there.

My second example is the following sentence from the biblical account of creation: "God formed man of dust from the ground, and breathed into his nostrils the breath of life" (Gen 2,7). —Just as in the case of the eschatological myths related by Plato's Socrates, the question which is crucial for all that follows is: Is this to be understood as "only a story" or as "information derived from a divine source"? The question remains the same; but the situation of the person who tries to answer it has changed fundamentally from that of Socrates. First, we have, in the meantime, such reliable information about the history of religions and cultures in general and about this text in particular that we can say, for example, that that biblical sentence merely reflects a notion of the origin of man which is typical in a primitive agrarian society. Information of this kind certainly does concern the theologian; but, of course, it is not theology. Second, paleontology and evolution research have brought to light such fundamental knowledge about the origin of man that we might be inclined to dismiss the biblical account of creation as something completely irrelevant in this day and age and to say that man is nothing more than an evolutionary phenomenon like fish and mammals. Again, it must be admitted that a theologian today cannot, of course, exempt himself from taking cognizance of the findings of those sciences and reflecting on them. However, this would not at all compel him to see the human spirit as nothing more than a phenomenon of evolution and the biblical account as an irrelevant story. But he will only understand the story if he believes it contains a message that transcends all that can humanly be known—an authentic divine message. But precisely in this point, with regard to the possibility of faith, the situation has radically changed from that of Plato's Socrates. Naturally it is not possible to speak about these things without bringing one's own fundamental convictions into play. The change here consists above all in the fact that a Christian, unlike Socrates, is no longer forced to refer to an unknown Prometheus, nor to the anonymous "ancient" figures, nor to the purely impersonal *logoi*, no matter how worthy of respect these are. Instead it is possible to have recourse to the Logos himself who has entered history and in whom the already mentioned *corpus mysticum* is personalized, which embraces the divine speaker and his witnesses and the believers. But as in the case of Socrates and Plato, entry into this community through which alone that affinity and *connaturalitas* take place by virtue of which a person is able to hear and to interpret what the supra-human author is saying through the text written by human hand—for example, that in the midst of the evolutionary process the human spirit is *not* something developing like everything else but is incomprehensibly a new reality which is not undergoing transition, and which does not "become,"[43] but emerges "finished" from its origin in the creator and remains directly connected with it. What is meant here can also be expressed as follows: true theology is only possible on the presupposition of self-inclusion in the *corpus mysticum*. Just as an unartistic person is not able to understand and interpret a poem, equally there cannot be a theologian who does not believe—provided that by theology we mean the attempt to give a valid interpretation of revelation.

Interpretation—by that is meant the task, which is now, of course, proving to be impossible to achieve once and for all, of understanding and making comprehensible what a person who makes utterances want to make known and to communicate.

---

43 Here Plato's notion that the soul is not only not transitory but something that has not become (agénetos; *Phaedrus* 246 a 11) takes on particular significance.

Theology and Pseudo-Theology

One cannot say what pseudo-theology is without measuring it against true theology. And so, what is theology? Traditionally it is defined as *doctrina secundum revelationem divinam* (doctrine according to divine revelation). Insofar as one sees it as a human undertaking, it is the attempt to interpret the divine revelation incorporated in the documents of sacred tradition with a view to finding out what is really meant. Perhaps someone will ask: what else could theology be if it is not "a human undertaking"? A counter question: Is it not feasible that the author of the revelation himself inspires the interpretation? For the Christian this is not only feasible, but rather he is convinced that in the interpretation of revelation by the Church this is precisely what happens. And so here alone is theology realized in the true sense of the word, as *doctrina sacra*. And if interpretation of a text means adequate investigation of what the author means, then it is not possible to think of a more perfect interpretation.

Because, of course, interpretation is always a sort of "translation"—carrying across meaning from one language into another—and because, furthermore, the original formulation of the divine message was done by the first recipient under the conditions of a past historical situation and because this same message has to be carried over into the likewise historically conditioned language of whatever present historical situation, theology is, whether carried out as interpretation of revelation by the Church itself or as the scholarly endeavor of individuals, a task which has to be performed ever anew. One can ask in what language a translator must be more

at home: in the language *into* which or in the language *from* which
he translates the text. In any case, the business of the theologian
necessarily requires "bilingualism." One could even envisage showing the two basic ways in which theology, which as interpretation
is always interpretation "of something for someone," has again and
again failed in its task because of inadequate command either of
the original language or of the current language. But, naturally,
more is required here than a purely linguistic competence. One
requisite is the complete modernity of the inner style, of the way
of thinking, of the mode of questioning and of the use of language;
another requisite is the ability to understand not only the vocabulary, the style and intonation of sacred text but also to hear,
through it, what cannot be fully and adequately expressed in any
historical language: the original word of the divine utterance as
"what is really meant." This latter is not something simply identi-
fiable in reality which could be "heard" in any given historical linguistic complex. Perhaps it is possible, for example, with regard to
the biblical report of the creation of man, to grasp and express
what is meant by it more purely—and to that extent "other"—than
before. We now know a little of the findings of evolution research.
The modern theologian cannot be unaware of evolution research
and paleontology if he is to be able to perform his own particular
theological task. This is only one of innumerable demands intrinsic
to real theology. And here it is clear that theology, strictly speaking—not unlike philosophy—by its very nature exceeds the capa-
bilities of any individual, no matter how gifted.

Still, it is possible to name conditions which absolutely must
be met if theology, in the strict sense, is to come about. It is never
the theologian's role as interpreter of revelation to find out, of himself, and "check" whether a divine utterance is real or not; nor is it
his role to say in which documents handed down God's statement
has been included. Instead, the theologian always presupposes not
only that God has spoken but also in what historical form the

revealing-revealed word has become accessible and perceptible to us. *A priori* to all theology this is already established, and indeed, "by someone else," namely by the authority at work in the *corpus mysticum* of the faithful. As Karl Jaspers says, this authority is essentially "uncomprehended." It is, accordingly, not validated by the documents which first have to be interpreted. Thus anyone who says he relies only on "Sacred Scripture" must face the question: how do you know that there is such a thing as sacred scripture and whether a particular book is part of its "canon" or not? And anyone who, as a theologian, is dealing with sacred scripture has *eo ipso* already accepted not only the fact of revelation but also the prior discovery of this fact. The act of the theologian implies both his faith and his own integration into the *corpus mysticum*. An "agnostic who knows his bible," as a modern Israeli called himself in conversation with me, can never be a theologian; and Bernanos has said it in a novel: to be a theologian without faith is "fraud."

Theological knowledge cannot be fruitful except as *cognition per connaturalities*, as knowledge based on fundamental solidarity, even loving identification, by virtue of which the infinite object appears not as something alien but as something which is directly one's own. Historical critical analysis, no matter how extensive, cannot make up for the lack of this fundamental affirmation although it can possibly make us forget it. On the other hand, the scholar who is dealing with the text in a similar way, though as a philologist, may develop out of this "engagement" an imaginative way of sensing and discovering which he might otherwise not have had. History, text criticism, and philology, as is quite obvious, are indispensable aids to theology; but they are not themselves theology. And when this non-theology nevertheless sees itself or presents itself as theology, or if it only more or less conceals its true character, then it becomes pseudo-theology. If it goes still further and claims, as a "branch of scholarship" which it truly is, to be the model for all meaningful treatment of the documents of revelation, then it leads, by confining the spirit to what can be known with scientific exactitude, precisely to that special form of intellectual unfreedom and narrowness that in any case threatens the man of science—perhaps only him—except that in the sphere of faith and theology it takes destruction and misery a step further. The ones who are most betrayed by such pseudo-theology are the students who are eager to learn but receive no warning and who, unfortunately when it is often too late, notice that their faith has been taken from them—not by an openly secularist philosophy of life, but, as Hegel puts it, "by the ravages of theology."

The Faith of Socrates

On what basis does Plato's Socrates "believe"? It is undoubtedly a question of faith when, for example, he is expecting judgement after death. In the whole corpus of Plato's work there is not even an attempt at a rational justification for this. There are arguments for the indestructibility of the soul, but for everything else that he has to say about life on the other side of death Plato has recourse to myth—information which, of course, does not stem from himself. He reports, but he is not the author—explicitly not. Socrates, and Plato as well, believes in this story handed down "from time immemorial," which comes at the conclusion of three great dialogs. "You think it is only a story, but I think it is truth. And the reason I relate it to you is that it is true," he says, for example, in "Gorgias." The person to whom he addresses this is Callicles, a powerful public figure schooled in sophistry, for whom fundamentally no argument has value except force. —The opinion that the myth of the Last Judgment is only a story is, as we know, widely subscribed to by scholars, and indeed the historian is able to produce much in support of this view. Only too well are we familiar with the origin of the highly diverse elements which are closely related here. The name *Minos* clearly points to Crete, where it was probably not a personal name at all but a general title for a king. And with regard to the fairness which is supposed to have qualified *Minos* to be a judge of the dead there are legends enough to contest this. From a completely different strand of tradition comes *Abacus*, to whom, strangely, the dead from Europe are assigned. The name *Abacus* occurs in the local folklore of Aegina, but it is also found in connection with the foundation of Troy. Besides, even the number of judges varies; on one occasion, three are named, another time four. Furthermore, it is extremely confusing to find, on closer examination, the numerous meanings of the name *Hades*, which refers both to a person and to a place; and the religious awe associated with the name seems to relate to the realm of the dead as well as to the fertility of the earth. And then, every Greek knows that *Acheron* is a river in Epirus and that its watercourse leads through rocky gorges and sometimes disappears under the earth's surface. And, finally, with regard to the "isles" of "the blessed," it can be shown that this is a misunderstood relic of the Minoan religion. And so on and so forth. One could bring to bear all the material contained in the "Realenzyklopädie der klassischen Altertumswissenschaft" to show that it is nothing but a story cobbled together from totally unrelated fragments—thus, a highly problematic affair.

What would Plato's Socrates have had to say in response? We need not wonder. In the "Phaedo" he says very clearly: naturally no reasonable person would insist that everything is exactly as it has been related. Neither the material from which the message is composed nor the form in which it is couched is a decisive factor. What is decisive is the message itself, which says: there is judgement after death. Only the message is important. This alone is what Socrates considers to be true, and indeed so true and valid that one can and must live one's life according to it. And so, again: on what basis does Socrates believe in the message about judgement after death? As we know, he has recourse to the "ancients" and to what has been said "from time immemorial." But it is completely clear that Plato does not immediately accept as a guarantee of its truth the pure fact that something has been handed down through the ages. The "ancients" are for him not just the "early" ones, those close to the origin. They are, above all, the first to receive "knowledge which has sprung from a divine source," and he believes them as witnesses to this divinely validated knowledge. But that means as well that he is in communion with the "ancients," although they remain nameless for him. As the theologian M. J. Scheeben says, whoever believes in another wants and achieves "spiritual union with him." "We believe because we love," as J. H. Newman says. Communion with the witnesses of truth is the required foundation for believing, whether for Socrates or for ourselves. Outside of this community which has been alive over the centuries faith has never been possible. The believer is always a member of this body which has been actively present in history. It is scarcely accessible empirically, this *corpus mysticum*—the name given to the Church from early times and which Karl Jaspers, vaguely enough, calls that "world of spirits" and which he says is "nowhere to be found objectively." —But if this is true, if the believer really believes on the basis of his being a member of this *corpus mysticum*, then we must ask: On what basis and in what way does this membership come about? How is it given to us?

Two Ways of Being "Critical"

There are clearly two ways of being "critical." The critical thinker is characterized, above all, by a certain watchfulness and care. This care is focused on ensuring that something which too easily happens to the uncritical mind does not also happen to himself. It is to be expected that in this the scientific researcher first comes to mind, for whom "being critical" means as much as taking care that only what has sufficiently been checked will be accepted as valid. But apart from science, which by its very nature has to do with facts which can be exactly established and are of a particular kind, there are other ways in which reality becomes accessible to us. In any case, as knowing beings we are not satisfied to know, for instance, the structure of the atom, in what way cancerous diseases come about, or, from the physiological point of view, what happens when a person dies. Instead, we insist on gaining at least some idea about the whole of reality and about our own existence. Our desire to know has as its aim what the English-American philosopher Alfred N. Whitehead calls "the complete fact," the big picture. In this we know quite clearly that there can never be exhaustive human knowledge of this "object" and that with the methods of the exact sciences the object can perhaps not even be focused on. And yet we are not deterred from asking about it and seeking an answer.

Above all, in philosophizing we are in this sense out after "the totality." That is precisely what philosophizing means: to question the totality of what we encounter in experience with regard to its ultimate meaning—a business which cannot be the preserve of a special academic discipline but one from which no one who desires to live under the impulse of a full intellectual life can dispense himself. But the believer—i.e., one who accepts as truth the divinely guaranteed message about the origin and goal of all creation—is also clearly concerned with the totality, the big picture.

In the normal course of events, philosophizing and believing are not uncritical, not up in the air. Neither the philosophizer nor the believer is allowed to ignore problems and counter arguments: both have the duty to be "critical," though each in his own way. They, too, are moved by the concern not to have something happen to them that can easily happen where there is uncritical thinking. This concern does relate to something completely different from that on which the watchfulness of the scientific researcher is focused, which is, in short, not to let anything slip through unchecked, whereas it is the duty of philosophizer and believer not to leave anything out and not to neglect anything that belongs to the totality of the world and that is meant for us and is spoken to us in the revelatory utterances of God. Rather than a possible loss of contact with reality they would—so that not the tiniest element of the totality of truth escape them—be ready to take the chance of achieving a lower degree of certainty. And as regards the believer, the words of John Henry Newman are worth remembering: that the critical concern of the believer is possibly manifested precisely in "not waiting for the most perfect possible proof."

Createdness:
The Elements of a Fundamental Concept
In Honor of the 700th Anniversary
of the Death of Thomas Aquinas

I

Thomas a Creatore, "Thomas of God the Creator"—so should the last great Master of the then still undivided Western Christendom be named, if one wanted to give him an added name following the example of the Carmelite Order ("John of the Cross"!): G. K. Chesterton makes this suggestion, almost casually, in his little book about Thomas Aquinas, an *opusculum* written in language which almost turned out to be journalistic—which did not deter a man of the caliber of Étienne Gilson to refer to it as "by far the best book" ever to have been written on the subject.[44] And in fact this comment, which puts the idea of creation and createdness at the center of Thomas's thinking about the world, hits the nail on the head. That the world, in its being, has the quality of something created, and that apart from the Creator God and his creature there can be no third reality—this is a conception which, naturally, in the whole of Christian theology has experienced many formulations. To have persevered with it and to have thought it through

44 See Maisie Ward, *Gilbert Keith Chesterton*. Regensburg 1956, pp. 532f.

to the end is something which distinguishes Thomas Aquinas, even amongst the great teachers of Christianity. —This statement includes two things. The first is that (contrary to the thesis of Marcion, which has expressly been taken up again in recent times, according to which the God of Christianity "has nothing to do with creation"[45]) the Creator is precisely not a *Deus extramundanus*,[46] but is closely bound up with creation and is at work in it: "God is necessarily in all things and indeed in the most intimate way."[47] The second is that the constitution and structure of the world that lies before our eyes, and of man himself, is completely determined by its nature as creature. It is precisely this fundamental concept of createdness, inexhaustible in its implications, of which I shall attempt to explain the elements in the following pages.

II

This undertaking could well begin with the analogy which compares created things—with regard to their structural form—with works produced by human beings, whether a technical apparatus or a product of art. The presupposition here is that the world of the human being in fact includes both: not only the *res artificiales*— things man produces himself—but also the *res naturales*, the reality he encounters which is independent of himself, what is created. At the same time, this presupposition does not seem to be simply obvious to contemporary thinking, since it was possible to write the following sentence: "The world is for man the objects he has produced himself and his social institutions."[48] But here I shall

---

45   See Anders Nygren, *Eros und Agape*. Gütersloh 1930, 1937.
46   See Herder's letter to Fr. Jacobi of 16.9.1785.
47   Thomas Aquinas, *Sum. Theol.* I, 8,1.
48   Peter Hacks, *Das Poetische*. Frankfurt 1972, p. 118.

leave aside this ideologically restricted view. With regard to the analogy between the things of nature understood as *creatura*—including, of course, the human being—and works of art, Thomas has often enough expressly used the formulation: "All created things are compared to God as the work of art is compared to man."[49]

It would be too easy if, like Jean-Paul Sartre, one were, in a hasty over-simplification to identify "production" and "creation," and ironically write off the traditional conception of creation as a "technical conception of the world," a *vision technique du monde.* [50] Not only does every human act of production—and in this it is fundamentally different from proper creation—presuppose something already existing and is therefore never "total-causality," simply bringing something into existence, in the strict sense making something exist; but the *res artificialis*, the work made by man, remains, precisely by virtue of its own existence received from elsewhere, independent of the producer in a way that is completely unthinkable in the relationship between God and creature. For this reason Thomas relativizes and supplements the analogy to the *artifex-artificatum* relationship by the addition of quite different images—by saying, for example, the creature is to God as the atmosphere is to the ray of sun which penetrates it and lights it up and which ceases to be lit up in the very same moment that the sun ceases to shine.[51] However, this does not in the least negatively affect the work of art analogy; one must only be aware of its limits. Strictly speaking, the concept of analogy itself suggests this, since it is a combination of similarity and dissimilarity, and clarity is only achieved when both are taken into account.

49 *Sum. Contra Gentiles* 2, 24; 3, 100.
50 J. P. Sartre, *L'existentialisme est un humanisme.* Paris 1946, p. 18.
51 *Sum. Theol.* I, 104,1; *Quaest. disp. de potentia Dei* 3, 3 ad 6.

III

What links the work created by man with the *creatura* in the strict sense is, above all, that both have the quality of being designed. Both are based on a plan. We can also say: both have come about in "what" they are (in their "essence," in their "nature") through the productivity of a creative intelligence, "through the knowledge of a knower."[52] Just as the "artificial" things made by man clearly stem from a human plan and a design, so it can be said of created things that they proceed from God "as known and intended."[53]

This fundamental quality—of being thought out and de-signed—has numerous implications and consequences for our thinking about the reality of the things that surround us and, above all, about man himself. Principally it means that man unavoidably has no say in what he is; he finds that he is this particular formed and defined person and that he does not make his nature himself. Our nature is, rather, essentially what is meant for us as creation. In a certain sense one can say it is what is meant for us by "someone else" and comes "from somewhere else." We owe it to none other than Jean-Paul Sartre, and the subtle radicality of his existentialist conception, that traditional thinking about man has been con-strained to remember the conceptual proximity and almost identity of "human nature" with "human createdness." Of course, Sartre does this by way of negation, or, more accurately, by the way he justifies the negation. Negation, which according to Sartre is "the first principle of existentialism," is this: "There is no human na-ture"; the basis for saying this: "... because there is no God who could have designed it."[54] Without doing violence to this idea we can also formulate it positively like this: it is only possible to speak

52   *Quaest. disp. de veritate* 3.3.
53   *Quaest. disp. de potentia Dei* 3.4.
54   *L'existentialisme*, p. 22.

of the nature of man if it is understood as something creatively designed by God. But this is expressly what Thomas Aquinas emphasizes where he says of the *formae*, the essences of things, that they are "nothing but the seal of divine knowledge, *quaedam sigillatio divinae scientiae in rebus.*"[55]

But this conception has several further implications—not just that man, because he is *creatura*, finds he has his own being as something given to him without his having a say, but also, for example, that for him, as for every creature, his nature is simply the first thing: the presupposition and the foundation of all his own decisions and actions and, in addition, of all other divine gifts he may receive. "What a being has by nature (*naturaliter*) is necessarily the foundation and principle of all else";[56] *naturalia praesupponuntur moralibus;*[57] *naturalia sund praeambula virtutibus gratuitis et acquisitis.*[58] —Implicit in this is something else which is hard to understand and which will be dealt with later: namely, that all that we want of our free will presupposes something that the will wants *on the basis of nature.*[59] But first another aspect must be dealt with.

IV

Everything that proceeds from the planned design of man has thereby the quality of what is in principle comprehensible; what comes about on the basis of human planning, no matter how much it is "materialized"—for example, as a machine and apparatus or a visual work of art—necessarily bears the marks of thought and

---

55 *Quaest. disp. de veritate* 2, 1 ad 6.
56 *Sum. Theol.* I, 82, 1.
57 *Quaest. disp. de correctione fraterna* I ad 5.
58 *Quaest. disp. de veritate* 16, 2 ad 5.
59 *Sum. Theol.* I, 10, 1 ad I.

can therefore be intelligible to the observer. A person with little knowledge of mathematics will possibly have no understanding of a computer system; however, for every one of the questions he may ask there is an answer which is understandable in itself and thereby shows the comprehensibility of the thing itself. —In exact analogy to this, the empirically verifiable comprehensibility of the world around us is grounded precisely on its being thought by the *Creator*. In any case, this is the only basis on which the possibility of deeper questioning becomes feasible. Moreover, we see this knowability of things, as also of human beings, not merely as a fact. We are clearly not able to think of something as real and at the same time as, in principle, not knowable. Charles C. Peirce goes so far as to say: "We cannot even talk about anything but a knowable object... The absolutely unknowable is a non-existent existence."[60] A university colleague, a logistics specialist, once asked me the critical question: "Would the sky fall in if it had to be admitted that there is a reality to which our knowing faculties have no possibility of access? Has physics not in fact, for example, already been confronted with such unknowable things in research about light?" In reply, I posed the counter-question whether the physicists had therefore finally abandoned their efforts at clarification. His answer: "No! Naturally not!" But does that not mean that everyone "naturally" supposes that what is for the time being not knowable has, on principle, the quality of knowability? Anyone who maintains that research into the as yet un-researched is meaningful is thereby affirming the intelligibility of the world. Outstanding scientists have, to their own surprise, noticed this truly astonishing fact—and spoken about it—as they reflect on the deeper presuppositions of their own discipline which are no longer "scientifically" comprehensible. I shall bring only two

60 *Collected Papers*. Vol.6. Harvard University Press 1960, p. 338; No. 492.

witnesses.[61] Albert Einstein says: "The most incomprehensible thing in nature is its comprehensibility." And it is Louis de Broglie who says: "We don't marvel enough at the fact that scientific knowledge is at all possible." Of course Gilson's addition to this is worth considering: that naturally "the question about possibility of science is not itself a scientific question."

I am fairly certain that the concept "the truth of things" never came to mind or was even familiar to either Einstein or de Broglie. They could hardly have been aware of it, since the concept—and even more so the expression "the truth of things"—was simply not found in the philosophical writings of this current period. It is true that in the twelfth century Anselm of Canterbury was already complaining that "the truth living *in* things is considered by few people."[62] But today it is a question of something different from the more or less chance non-use of a particular set of concepts or terminology; the concern is about the result of a long process of suppression and omission. Here the open polemical rejection (for example, by Bacon, Hobbes, Spinoza) was probably less significant than the progressive falsification and hollowing out of the original meaning—above all in the philosophy of the German Enlightenment (A. G. Baumgarten, Christian Wolff). All of this eventually gave Immanuel Kant apparent justification for saying that the proposition that every being is "true" (*omne ens est verum*) is tautological and sterile and to eliminate the formulation "truth of things" from philosophical vocabulary.[63] But what is meant by "the truth of things," as we have said, is, most precisely, that ontological

---

61 Both quoted in Etienne Gilson, Philosophy and Religious Wisdom. In: *Proceedings of The American Catholic Philosophical Association*. Vol. 26. Washington 1952, p. 9.

62 *Dialog about Truth*, ch.9.

63 See Josef Pieper, *Wahrheit der Dinge*. 4th impression. Munich 1966, pp. 16ff.

light character of nature—discovered with astonishment and identified by Albert Einstein and Louis de Broglie—and of all other
reality, which puts it in range of our knowing. This lucidity which
is characteristic of all reality can only be plausible to one who sees
the world as *creatura* and who, for example, accepts Augustine's
statement in the final chapter of his "Confessions": *"We* see things
because they are; but they are, because You see them."[64]

Precisely that is what is meant by "the truth of things": it ap-
pertains to the constitution of the reality of the world as a whole
to be "placed between two knowing subjects, *inter duos intellectus*,
between the—in the strict sense—creative knowing mind of the
divinity and the reliving mind of the creature;[65] and only on this
basis is the world accessible to our human knowing faculties so that
we can know that He has known them as Creator and has designed
them. And this is also the only basis for understanding the notion
of "word character" (R. Guardini[66]) and the notion of "the language of things," by virtue of which the character of "hermeneutic"
is justly, and in a precise sense, attributed to all philosophical interpretation of reality—hermeneutics seen as the interpretation of
word communications. Hans-Georg Gadamer was the one who,
with great clarity, pointed to the link of "the language of things"
with its metaphysical root by saying: "... it is their quality as creature that links soul and thing";[67] "the essence and reality of creation
itself consists in being such an accord between soul and thing."[68]
However, this is, as immediately becomes clear, unfortunately only
meant in the sense of an historical description, a respectful

---

64 *Confessions* 13, 38.
65 *Quaest. disp. de veritate* I,2.
66 Romano Guardini, *Welt und Person*. Würzburg 1940, p. 110.
67 Hans-Georg Gadamer, *Kleine Schriften*, vol. I. Tübingen 1967, pp.
    63f.
68 Ibid., p. 64.

representation of an argumentation that was at one time possible. A person philosophizing today, says Gadamer, "certainly can no longer use such a theological argument."[69] Here we must first pose the critical question whether acceptance of the creation character of world and man is a strictly theological supposition, i.e., one which presupposes a link with revelation and faith; Plato and Aristotle, who, though they did not formally have the concept of *creatio ex nihilo*, came very close to it, can still be cited as an important counter argument. Second, it must likewise be said: if the argument from createdness is not acceptable there is no ultimately feasible explanation for the at first "incomprehensible" fact, as Einstein calls it, that reality can at all be grasped by human knowledge; and what Gadamer has so convincingly shown as the chance of understanding is frustrated. The same image of the cul-de-sac can be found, shamefully, in some of the new scholasticism textbooks, which, it is true, no differently from the school metaphysics of the seventeenth and eighteenth centuries, respectfully (as Kant says) use the term "the truth of things" ("ontological truth") but without its original meaning because it was embarrassing for them to have recourse to the category of creation which is now seen as "unphilosophical." And so it is to be welcomed that again and again, outside of the territory of academic philosophy, we are put on the right path by men like Einstein and de Broglie or by a man like Günter Eich—an author who reflects on the dimension from which poetic language originates. Although, as he says himself, he is in constant "opposition to the establishment, not only in society but in the whole of creation,"[70] he confesses, in his reflections during a speech made to people blinded in war, that the important thing is that "everything written should be approaching theology,"

---

69 Ibid.
70 Quoted from H.-J. Heise, *Günter Eich zum Gedenken*. Neue Rundschau. No. 84 1973, p. 176.

by which he means precisely the necessary reference of the literary word to the creator's original word incorporated in reality: "Every word retains a reflection of the magical condition where it is identical with creation. From this language—never heard and not audible—it is as if we can only translate as best we can and in any case always imperfectly. What is really crucial about writing is that we have the task of translating; that is what makes writing difficult and sometimes perhaps even impossible."[71] The element of resignation in these last words indicates another essential point which we now need to deal with.

V

The original creative word incorporated in the reality of the world can never be adequately "translated" into the vocabulary of human language, whether in literature, science, or philosophy. The impossibility is to be explained by the fact that that "original word"—although things derive their lucidity from it—is not completely *audible* to the created mind. Einstein does say that nature is "comprehensible"; but here we have to speak more precisely—distinguishing between "knowing" and "comprehending." Not all knowing is also comprehending. Only the highest and most intense realization of knowing is called, in the strict sense, "comprehending." It is a knowing that exhausts its object. Here Aquinas gives a very clear definition: "It is said that a person comprehends a thing in the proper sense when he knows it as well as it is knowable in itself."[72] But this statement is based on the conviction that it is in the nature of created things that their knowability can never be exhausted by a finite knowing faculty and transformed into the

---

71   Susannne Müller-Hanpft (editor), *Über Günter Eich*. Frankfurt 1970, pp. 23f.

72   *Commentary on St. John's Gospel* I, 11.

state of being known—because the basis for its total knowability is at the same time the basis for its incomprehensibility. All created beings are, insofar as we are really talking about *them*, of themselves perceptible and visible (just as the stars, even in the bright light of day—insofar as we are talking about themselves and their quality—are equally "visible" as they are in a clear night sky); things are knowable because they are *creatura*. But it must be said as well: because they are *creatura* they are unfathomable for human knowing faculties, which are not capable of achieving a fundamental grasp of the design of things that lives in the creative Logos and by virtue of which they are visible. This is what is meant by the formulation used by Aquinas in many variations: *Rerum essentiae sunt nobis ignotae*, "the essences of things are unknown to us."[73] This formulation is, of course, only seldom found in the textbooks of the schools which invoke his authority.

It is easy to see that this conception, which implies a whole view of the world, has nothing at all to do with agnosticism, and of course still less—something which is occasionally overlooked—with the rationalism of the "closed systems" or also of "the epistemological optimism of Marxist philosophy"[74] which has been formally adopted by and integrated into the official doctrine of Bolshevism, according to which there is nothing which is unfathomable but only "things which are *not yet* known."[75] —In fact, this rationalism is not so much a statement about the quality of

73 *Quaest. disp. de veritate* 10, 1.—Commentary on Aristotle's "On the Soul" I,1; no. 15.—Quaest. disp. de spiritualibus creaturis II ad 3.— *Quaest. disp. de veritate* 4, 1 ad 8.

74 Thus "the first comprehensive German textbook of Marxist-Leninist philosophy." See *Marxistische Philosophie*. Berlin 1967, p. 519; 524.

75 Friedrich Engels, *Ludwig Feuerbach und der Ausgang der klassischen deutschen Philosophie*. Berlin 1946, pp. 17f. See also J. M. Bocheński, *Der sowjetrussische dialektische Materialismus*. Bern-Munich 1950, p. 95.

objective reality as about human reason, to which the capacity for "exhaustive knowledge"[76] is expressly attributed.

It is probably not possible to say that the unfathomable nature of things can be "empirically verified" in the same way as their knowability, but it seems to me significant that precisely the statements of scientists who are particularly distinguished for their "exact" research insist on this unfathomability. It is Albert Einstein who calls the comprehensibility of nature something incomprehensible and, furthermore, without in the least wanting to cast doubt on findings of modern physics, writes, a few weeks before his death: "If there is one thing I have learnt in the ponderings of a long life it is this: that we are much further removed from a deeper insight into elementary processes than most of our contemporaries think."[77] And it is Alfred North Whitehead, the co-author of *Principia Mathematica*, who says about the "simple" fundamental philosophical question *What is it all about?* that all of our human experience tells us that it "cannot be answered once and for all."[78]

VI

"It is not how things are in the world that is mystical, but that it exists"—this is what Ludwig Wittgenstein says in his "Tractatus Logico-philosophicus."[79] The sentence is clearly not far removed from the old question which Heidegger was by no means the first to formulate: "Why is there anything at all, why is there not

---

76 Fr. Engels, *Ludwig Feuerbach und der Ausgang der klassischen deutschen Philosophie*, p. 17.

77 In a letter to Max von Laue 3.2.1955 (published in the *Frankfurter Allgemeine Zeitung* of 23.4.1955).

78 Remarks. In: *The Philosophical Review*. Vol. 46; 1937, p. 178.

79 *Tractatus Logico-philosophicus* 6, 44.

nothing?"[80] It is clear that these utterances concern not the what-ness, the *essentia* of things in reality, but formally their *existentia*, their actual presence in the world. And further: just as the "nature" which every finite being has is based on the planning and knowing of the Creator, so too the factual existence of a clearly not-absolute, "contingent" being can only be accounted for by recourse to a cre-ator's will—which is absolutely free and for that very reason not completely comprehensible by human reason, and which is the cre-ator of existence. Here again we can be grateful for the enlighten-ing radicality of Jean-Paul Sartre who declares that an existence that is obviously not necessary but is also not backed by an absolute will is simply "absurd." He is completely correct (and moreover is repeating, the other way round and possibly without realizing it, the old argument for the existence of God which Hegel[81] was still using and which was likewise based on the *contingentia mundi*.) The alternative we are discussing here can fairly exactly be character-ized in the terms used by Sartre and Wittgenstein: either "absurd" or "mystical"; one could also, staying partly with Sartre's vocabu-lary, say: either arousing "disgust" or being attractive. Just as the "ontic" truth of things, their knowability and lucidity, are due to their being thought by the Creator, so too the creative will is the basis of their affirmation, and therefore of their being good, as a quality inherent in their being—so that the variant form of the

---

80   Thus F. W. J. Schelling in his *Philosophie der Offenbarung* (Werke 13, p. 243). Leibniz says something similar shortly before his death in the tract written as a legacy (see *Philosophische Schriften*. Ed. H. H. Holz, vol. 1. Darmstadt 1965, p.410) for Prince Eugen on the Prinzipien der Natur und der Gnade: *Pourquoi il y a plustôt quelque chose que rien?* (Ibid., p. 426). For the whole complex of questions see Anna Teresa Tymieniecka, *Why is there something rather than noth-ing?* Assen (Holland) 1966.

81   *Vorlesung über die Beweise vom Dasein Gottes* (1829). Ninth lecture, towards the end.

passage from Augustine quoted above would be entirely valid: *Our love is first ignited by the goodness of what we love; but what we love is good because God loves and affirms it*. When we, turning in love to another person, exclaim: It's wonderful that you *are!*—then this approval is only possible and authentic because it is a *re*affirmation and, all things being well, perhaps also the continuation and completion of the divine begetting in love that has preceded it, which, in the act of *creatio*, has, in a wonderful way,[82] given to everything its existence and goodness. And if "celebrating a feast" means as much as, on a particular occasion and in the not usual way, living out the affirmation of the world and of existence[83]—how, in the middle of the confusion and worry of workaday life, could any kind of celebration be considered real if that affirmation were not based on the created goodness of reality and existence, or, in other words, if it were not true to say *omne ens est bonum*.

Precisely this fundamental, wise statement which says not only that all being is good but also that, despite everything, it is good for man to exist—this proposition, which has been largely degraded to a sterile textbook existence, has inevitably lost the spice of existential relevance and every acceptable meaning, if the world and man are not seen as *creatura*, and existence, above all one's own, as in the strictest sense created: i.e., as an existence caused by a creative act of affirmation.

And we can take for granted that it is of some importance for a person's existence in the world whether or not he is able to experience himself as something absolutely affirmed—as *creatura*. Of

---

82 See the age-old prayer which until recently occurred in the Roman Mass liturgy which said about God that He wondrously created man and then still more wondrously created him anew.

83 See Josef Pieper, *Zustimmung zur Welt. Eine Theorie des Festes.* 2nd impression Munich 1964, p. 52.

necessity this would mean that his feeling about his existence bears this fundamental stamp. Perhaps we should be reminded of Spinoza's fearsome world view hidden in the sentence, "Strictly speaking, God loves nobody,"[84] in order to become aware of the incredibly different view, that our own existence consists literally in being loved by the Creator. An author who is now forgotten wrote, in a similarly forgotten but significant book and in an old-fashioned celebratory mode, about what this can mean *in concreto* for human self-understanding: "Since God loves me because I am, I am irreplaceable in the world."[85] I think there is no other way for us, even in our own consciousness, to find our feet once and for all than through such a conviction—which, of course, cannot simply be achieved merely by a decision on our part. Only on the basis of this certainty of being loved in an absolutely positive way can that sense of fundamental trust be established, by virtue of which a person is able to live unproblematically—and "simply," in the biblical sense. And if people today speak so insistently on the danger of "loss of identity" the question has to be asked whether this danger could not be averted precisely through the experience of existing as someone irrevocably wanted by God himself. Anyway, compared with the stability of this foundation the oft-vaunted "being down to earth" seems to be on very shaky ground.

VII

But this iron indestructibility of that which has proceeded from the will of the Creator who placed it in existence has further aspects. It can, for example, be turned against created things, and we may be reminded of the, at first, unsettling words of Plato's

---

84 *Ethica*, 5; propos. 17, corollarium.
85 Ladislaus Grünhut, *Eros und Agape. Eine metaphysisch-religion-sphilosophische Untersuchung*. Leipzig 1931, p. 20.

Socrates, that precisely immortality is a "terrifying danger"[86]—for the one who does not want the good. In creation something happens which simply cannot be reversed. "No created being can simply be called 'transitory.'"[87] Once called into existence the creature can never completely disappear from reality—even if the creature itself wanted, in a momentary impulse, to seek self-extinction and a return to nothingness. There is no need to discuss whether these days such an impulse is a familiar experience.

But the condition of existing as a creature, as we need to discuss it here, is a much more complicated thing. We can only describe it in sentences which seem to contradict one another. On the one hand, creation says: God does not keep being for himself but communicates it to the creature in such a way that it is the creature's own property. Thus it is possible to speak meaningfully of finite things without necessarily having to speak of God. When Werner Heisenberg says that for medieval thinking it was "meaningless to ask questions about the material world independently of God"[88] we have to make the critical comment that (for example) Aquinas maintained exactly the contrary: "The creature can be considered without reference to God."[89] At the same time, it is undeniably true that created beings are totally incapable, of themselves, of keeping themselves in existence, so that, looked at absolutely, they can indeed be "turned back to nothingness."[90] And yet the creature, especially the spiritual creature, has to be called in a strict sense indestructible, "not able not to be,"[91] nor to do substantial damage to the "nature" given to it as its own in the act of creation.

86 *Phaedo*, 107 c 4.
87 Thomas Aquinas, *Commentary on the Sentences* I d. 8,3,2.
88 Werner Heisenberg, Das Naturbild der heutigen Physik. In: *Die Künste im technischen Zeitalter*. Darmstadt 1956, p. 32.
89 *Commentary on the Sentences* 3 d. 11, 1 ad 7.
90 *Sum. Theol.* III, 13, 2.
91 *Commentary on Aristotle's Metaphysics* 10, 12; no. 2145.

Nihilism, by contrast, according to which we could and should take the step into nothingness, is only the pain and despair side of the idealism regarding our similarity with the divine to which it sees itself opposed. "The capability not to be does not reside in created beings; but rather in God there resides the power to give them being or to make the flow of being dry up in them."[92] Only the Creator could call back created beings into nothingness: *Sicut solus Deus potest creare, ita solus potest creaturas in nihilum redigere.*[93] Although the idea already expressed in the Bible (Gen 6, 6)—that in the face of the unending abuse of creation by man such an annihilation could be an act of divine justice—seems to have occurred to Aquinas,[94] he nevertheless clings ultimately to the likewise biblical information that God, in His wisdom, "created all things *so that they might be* (Wisdom I, 14) and not that they should sink back into nothingness."[95]

VIII

"All activity of the will leads back, as if to its earliest root, to that which, by his very nature, man wills."[96] This idea, which at first seems difficult for us to grasp, is an indispensable and intrinsic element of the notion "createdness"—to the extent that this notion means that God has, in his Creator's plan, given his creature a particular "nature" and has meant something by it prior to any shaping undertaken by the creature himself; but also to the extent that, again without being asked, the creature has been brought into existence by an absolute act of the creator's will: i.e., has been set on

92 *Sum. Contra Gentiles* 2, 30; also *Sum. theol.* I, 75, 6 ad 2.
93 *Sum. Theol.* III, 13, 2.
94 *Quaest. disp. de potentia Dei* 5,4 ad 6; *Commentary on the Sentences* 4 d. 46, 1, 3 ad 6.
95 *Quaest. quodlibetales* 4, 4.
96 *Quaest. disp. de caritate*; similarly *Sum. theol.* I, II, 10, 1.

the path of fulfilment that has not only been "thought of" for him but also "willed" for him. Heidegger's notion of "thrownness"[97] [into existence] would therefore not be so wide of the mark if it included the notion of the "thrower" and his creative affirmative power, and if in this way the dark and tragic connotations of this term were to disappear. In fact, this prime act of *creatio* is—in line with Leibniz's thinking[98]—to be conceived of as a "fulguration," an incomparably "explosive" process from which all created dynamism received its impulse and has been kept in motion.

For anyone accustomed to think of "nature" and "spirit" as mutually exclusive concepts it is understandably almost impossible to think that there could be a willing—a spiritual act *per definitionem*— which unfolds like an event in the natural world. But the great teachers in Christendom have always contested the idea that "nature" and "spirit" are opposed to one another in this way. Instead, they have tenaciously clung to their opinion that there is, at any rate, *one* kind of being, namely the created spirit, in which both are united: nature and spirit. To put it differently: as soon as man is understood as *creatura* there is not the slightest difficulty in accepting—on the contrary it is quite obvious—that in the spiritual core of human existence something can happen, and must happen, that, on the one hand, by virtue of creation and therefore as a natural process is independent of us, yet, on the other hand, stems from the middle of our spirit and therefore can only be thought of as a spiritual act. In this link, which can only be made plausible if we presuppose the createdness of man, we have the only possibility of establishing a common root for two contrasting interpretations of human willing: the "determinist" and its opposite, both partly (but only partly!) supported empirically. As we know from totally

---

97 "... this 'that it is' we call the *thrownness* of this being into its There." Martin Heidegger, *Sein und Zeit*. Tübingen 1949, p. 135.
98 Leibniz, *Monadologie*, § 47.

reliable experience that we are capable of making free decisions
("Wherever there is intellectual knowledge there is also freedom
to decide"[99]), there is equally compelling evidence from experience
that we "want" our own final fulfilment with the same "natural"
willing as the falling stone "wants" to go down;[100] that "wanting
to be happy is not a question of free decision."[101] —Because we are
created spirit, not to be satisfied except with good as a whole, the
bonum universale,[102] we are not determined (fixed), but free in our
choice when faced with particular good things which can only be
characterized as means to an end but not as *the* end. But because
we are at the same time "created" spirit, sent in the act of *creatio*
on the way to our own perfection without our being asked, we
therefore want this perfection "on the basis of our being created,"
and that means by nature and not by virtue of our own choice. But
it is at the very least problematic to speak here of "determination";
it can be accurate or inaccurate. It is accurate to speak of "determination" if by this term we mean that the will is fixed in one particular direction. But if it is taken to mean "determined from
outside" this is already a distortion and falsification, for it belongs
to the concept of natural will that this is an impulse arising from
the inner core of the willing subject; the natural drive for happiness
is bound up with his most fundamental willing. And if being free
means being able to act without being impeded by any external
limiting factor, we have freedom in the strict sense. Of course, it
remains true that this natural willing points back—even if it goes
through the human heart—to an ultimate source which is not
human but supra-human. For this reason it is not in man's power

99 *Sum. Theol.* I, 59, 3.
100 Ibid., I, II, 13, 6; *Sum. contra Gentiles* 3, 4.
101 *Sum. Theol.* I, 19, 10.
102 Nihil potest quietare voluntatem hominis nisi bonum universale.
     Sum. theol. I, II, 2, 8.

to will anything else. And if, therefore, being free means being able to choose and to do something else, then in this case there is *no* freedom. — It is not possible to reduce this issue to a simple formula. Even Aquinas's energy for achieving conceptual clarity did not manage to go beyond saying: "Will seeks happiness in freedom although it seeks it out of necessity!"[103] Clearly, the concept of freedom appears in a different light when seen in conjunction with the notion of createdness.

Anyone who, again like Jean-Paul Sartre, systematically denies that man is *creatura* and that there is therefore no human nature presupposed as existing prior to all of our decisions, has to reckon with a detachment in which supposedly the whole 360-degree range of the compass rose is open, which at the same time involves total lack of orientation—because then logically "man has no possible support either in himself or outside of himself"[104]: "there are no signs in the world."[105] This is precisely that famous kind of freedom to which one is not called but condemned"[106] and which is almost identical with despair. ("This word has an extremely simple meaning: that we limit ourselves to relying on that which depends on our willing."[107]) All of this is, fairly exactly, the negative side of truth and needs only to be translated into its opposite for it to become clear to anyone thinking impartially about the depths of human existence that a life in freedom—secure against despair and disorientation—is only possible where man accepts and affirms with all its consequences the fact that his own nature has been given to him: i.e., where he affirms his own createdness.

103 *Quaest. disp. de potentia Dei* 10, 2 ad 5; similarly, referring to Augustine (*City of God* 5, 10), in *Sum. Theol.*: "Necessity arising from nature does not cancel freedom of the will" (I, 82, I ad 1).
104 *L'existentialisme*, p.36.
105 Ibid., p. 47.
106 Ibid., p. 37.
107 Ibid., p. 49.

IX

To conclude these already aphoristic remarks, some further aspects of the many-sided concept of "createdness" must at least be named, if not dealt with.

"As long as it was possible to believe that the world was created by a reason comparable with human reason but of an absolutely high degree" it was possible to think of the whole world as unified in itself and homogenous";[108] but, for an ontology "treading new paths," such a conception is considered to be "no longer an image of the real world";[109] instead, "reason's need for unity is seen to be illusory."[110] This thesis formulated by Nicolai Hartmann is both problematic and worth considering. It seems problematic—quite apart from his assigning to the past any belief in creation—to think that the "old" ontology, "the doctrine of being which was dominant from the time of Aristotle down to the end of the era of scholasticism,"[111] "denied multiplicity" and saw the world as simply homogenous. That is an inadmissible simplification. Thomas Aquinas, for example, understands precisely the colorful variety of things expressly as "not coming about by chance"[112] but as something necessarily bound up with the essence of creation;[113] it is the unity of the universe itself that demands the difference of its parts.[114] Such unity and uniqueness of the world—and this is what is worth considering in Nicolai Hartmann's idea—cannot be more convincingly proven than by reference to its character as creation. "Just as

108 Nicolai Hartmann. *Neue Wege der Ontologie*. Stuttgart 1947, p. 245.
109 Ibid., p. 240.
110 Ibid., p. 245.
111 Ibid., p. 203.
112 *Compendium theologiae* I, 102.
113 *Sum. Theol.* I, 47, 1.
114 *Quaest. disp. de potentia Dei* 3, 16 ad 1.

God is one, he has produced a one thing [*unumquodque*]; not only is each being one in itself, but all things are in a certain sense "a one thing" which is perfect.[115] And just as Nicolai Hartmann distanced himself from reason's supposedly "illusory" need of unity and from the notion—which makes no sense to Hartmann—of the world as *creatura*, Thomas declares it as simply necessary that all things belong to *one* world; and he, too, adds a—so to speak—historical reflection on the past: it would follow that only "those could suppose that there are several worlds who have not seen that the world originates from a wisdom that creates order."[116] Besides, there is the question whether the assumption of a fundamentally un-unified reality would not also have incalculable consequences for man's self-understanding as a point of convergence of several spheres of being—not to mention that the notion of an intrinsically disparate world as well as of a reality that is in principle incomprehensible cannot seriously be thought and sustained.

Moreover, the notion of the createdness of all things, even though it may perhaps be—as something in fact realized—foreign to modern consciousness, has left such a mark on our thinking, like some secret ingredient, that consistent denial of it possibly and perhaps unexpectedly unsettles things which we have never expressly associated with the world seen as creation. For example, we might suppose that the attitude towards the world as a whole (silent listening), which the Greeks have called *theoria* and which is primarily concerned with things showing themselves as they are—it has also been called the attitude specific to philosophizers—we

---

115 Ibid. "Ad primum ergo dicendum, quod sicut Deus est unus, ita et unum produxit, non solum quia unumquodque in se est unum, sed etiam quia omnia quodammodo sunt unum perfectum, quae quidem unitas diversitatem partium requirit, ut ostensum est."
116 *Sum. Theol.* I, 47, 3.

might suppose that that contemplative[117] attitude can only be sustained and deemed in harmony with one's own sense of values on the following condition: that the object of such "purely theoretical" philosophical questioning, directed to truth[118] and nothing else—i.e., to reality—is considered as something quite different from the matter and raw material of a praxis geared towards meeting our daily needs. This contemplative attitude is, as is to be expected, constantly endangered and even discredited by a utilitarian attitude which tends to assert its dominance. The philosophical *theoria* as an attitude can probably only be lived insofar as and as long as the world is understood as something meaningful and grounded in a supra-human reality—as something worthy of our reverence and itself in a certain sense divine: in a nutshell, insofar as and as long as the world is understood as *creatura*.

Although creation as a process and event necessarily remains inaccessible to our knowing faculties, still it can be said that it must be at any rate a non-temporal event which transcends all succession in time and is unrelated to time. By seeing man and the world as creation, I have, consciously or otherwise, taken it that my own existence and historical existence as a whole not only "borders" directly on the region of the eternal but is completely saturated with eternity. And so, "transcending time," although, of course, not something we can simply choose at will, is one of our real human possibilities. Our repeated awareness of going beyond the "here and now" in an inchoate way in artistic experience but above all in prayer and in the solemn celebration of real feasts—such transcending of our actual existence, limited as it is by space and time, to a greater world which is out there for us some time in the future,

---

117 Theoria, id est contemplatio—that is the Latin translation on which Aquinas bases his Commentary on Aristotle's *Metaphysics* (2, 1; 993 a 30).

118 Aristotle, *Metaphysics* 993 b 20.

will appear as unreal and as a poetic idealization only to those who do not see or admit to the true situation of man within the whole of reality; but for anyone who accepts and considers the createdness of man, the thought that our existence unfolds in a "doublehoused" sphere of existence is nothing other than the simple description of reality.

All of these considerations are not quite the concern of theology as such—seen as the attempt to interpret the revelatory words of God and the sacred tradition based on it. However, the sphere of the "supernatural" in the strict sense is not something separated from the nature of concrete persons; instead, the ontological openness of our being with regard to revelation, grace, and sacrament is not itself "supernatural," for it, too, comes as a gift with the birth of the finite spirit (*naturaliter anima est gratiae capax*[119]). This is already clearly included in the concept of createdness. Because being a creature means continually receiving one's own being from the divine origin and being continuously created, creatures do not cease—despite the individuality they enjoy precisely through *creatio*—to be always prepared for a new intervention on the part of the *creator* (a preparedness which the teachers in Christendom have called *potentia oboedientiae*[120]). This "potency" is based on the fact that the creature—by contrast with works which are at a certain point "finished" by human beings—remains forever "clay in the hands of the potter." And so there is also a false "supernaturalistic" notion of the supernatural character of faith, grace, and sacrament, which can only be avoided by one who has the right concept of man's createdness. *Being able* to believe is, as Augustine says,[121] part of man's nature; and, insofar as unbelief is the refusal to accept a communication from God

119 *Sum. Theol.* I, II, 113,10.
120 *Sum. Theol.* III, 11, 1—Quaest. disp. de veritate 8, 12 ad 4—Quaest. disp. de potentia Dei 6, 1 ad 18.
121 De praedestinatione Sanctorum, cap. 5, 10. Migne *PL* 44, 968.

that has become sufficiently perceptible, it not only violates a norm which has a purely supernatural justification, but it also contradicts what man is by virtue of creation; unbelief is, seen in this light, contrary to his nature,[122] which is the nature of a created being.

*

By way of a kind of coda, an analogy might be used to show how indispensable it is for reflection on our own roots to remain consistently aware of the category "createdness." In the sphere of Western civilization it is clear that everyone, whether he knows it or not, in fact speaks Latin and Greek. Even someone who on a daily basis reads in the newspaper about aggression and atomic energy, about repressive tolerance and integration, about anti-cyclical economic measures, about methods and programs, is constantly dealing with these two languages. A person can undoubtedly, even though not knowing a single original word of the language of Cicero or Augustine or indeed Plato and the New Testament, handle such terms and make himself understood by using them. However, the question can be asked whether someone can justifiably be called educated who only half understands what he is saying himself. — It is the same, I think, with regard to the concept of creation and its elements. It determines not only the foundation and structure of the world and of existence but also the actual, largely unreflected but undeviating thinking of man—and not just Christian man— about reality. Of course, conceptual clarification can be reasonably achieved here without consciously having recourse to the category "createdness." But anyone who wants to measure up to the demands of radical thinking can hardly be dispensed from using it. Otherwise he would have to face the reproach that he understands only the half of what he is thinking.

122 Infidelitas ... est contra naturam. *Sum. theol.* II, II, 10, 1 ad 1.

Sartre's Proof for the Existence of God

The clearest argument for the existence of God that has been formulated in our day comes from none other than Jean-Paul Sartre, and it is not only completely "modern" but also totally "existential." —Sartre makes two presuppositions. The first is, as everyone knows, the thesis of the non-existence of God. Although it is not supported by one single argument, it is straightforwardly stated as a presupposition. The other presupposition is the very directly and intensely experienced non-necessity of the world. "Existence is not necessary"; "the essential is fortuitous." This is the insight which comes to Antoine Roquentin, the hero of the novel "La Nausée" when he looks around the park—at the trees, at the fountain, and, above all, at himself. "We were a little pile of existing things that felt embarrassed; we didn't have the slightest reason for being there." "Everything that exists is born without a reason, lives on in his weakness, and dies through an external cause." All right, one could say, is that any different from a (somewhat aggressive) but completely accurate description of the "contingency" of the world? Is that not what has always been said: nothing that we encounter in our experience "must" exist? So what is new? It seems to me that what is new is that Sartre does not accept this contingency. "I was afraid, but above all: I was raging; I found it so stupid, so misplaced"; "I felt helpless rage"; "when you become clear about this it turns your stomach: that is disgust [Nausée]"; "It is absurd that we were born; it is absurd that we die." "I had experienced everything about existence. I went back into my hotel and wrote it down."

But is not that what is meant by the old "proof of God's existence" which Hegel in his later years calls the argument *e contingenia mundi*? What else is being said here—in both cases—if not that an unnecessary, "contingent" being that "does not sustain itself" (Hegel) is indeed nonsense, inconceivable, crazy, unbearable, absurd—unless it is thought of in conjunction with a necessary and existing absolute which is the foundation of being that sustains it: namely, God. But could it not, however, be possible that man and the world around him have no meaning and are therefore fundamentally absurd? Two things have to be said in answer to this. First, it is not possible for anyone to persevere in this thought process; one can think it but not live it. Even Sartre cannot manage it. How else could he speak of responsibility and freedom, and on what basis could he distinguish between right and wrong? Second, if one really wants to attempt being consistent in this, would that not mean that there simply could not be a "foundation" for anything, not even a "foundation" for maintaining the non-existence of God?

The blind spot in the eye is the point where the optic nerve is found. The fact seems to me particularly useful as an analogy for the mind, the human knowing faculties: because created, the mind is not able to achieve a full and complete explanation and grasp of the self. Irreducible and indissoluble, the spirit is firmly fixed in the foundation of its being as if by a blind root and navel—a foundation which is not identical with the spirit. It is not given to the finite spirit to be clear about this root and to subsume it into the self; it is not possible to get behind the root of its own being. There is no retina (not even in the spirit—insofar as we are talking about a finite spirit) which can see everything around it; somewhere there is a blind spot. And that is precisely the point where the organ of sight emerges. Precisely because created being is made possible by something outside itself there has to be a blind spot. (1947)

The sentence "Agendo patimur esse" *which, as a twenty-three-year-old I thought up and noted down, taking particular pleasure in the succinct formulation, still holds today. In and through our activity we bear our existence. That includes, first, the fact that being is a gift to us, i.e., that we do not account for it ourselves; second, that it is only given to the active person—and in the measure that he is active.* (1942)

Sign and Symbol as the
Language of Christian Faith

I thought at first that the theme posed for me in this formulation would require something approaching a "timeless" academic essay. And there are, in fact, things which do need conceptual clarification. But looking at it again and more closely, it became clear to me that what is being considered here is of real contemporary concern: whether, and in what way in this current period—where almost everything seems to be technically achievable, and only producing and the producible are of any real significance–whether and in what way the feeling for sign and symbol can be kept alive and strengthened in man, even Christian man; perhaps it even has to be awakened or at least reawakened, not just for the sake of some kind of enriching of cultural and intellectual life—some sort of topping up—but because, to put it briefly, we are here concerned with *praeambula sacramenti*. At first, this formulation sounds somewhat strange by comparison with the term *praeambula fidei*, by which we mean the intellectual presuppositions which must be fulfilled if acceptance, in faith, of a divine revelation of truth is to be deemed possible. And we immediately see, without any difficulty, that such faith is only feasible when, explicitly or implicitly, there is the conviction that (for example) God exists at all as one capable of speaking and possibly also revealing himself. But this conviction is not already included in what the believer believes, but rather it is a presupposition of his belief; it is found, so to speak, in the "court-yard" of the temple but not in the temple itself; it belongs, in the formulation of Western theology, not to the *articuli fidei* but precisely to the *praeambula ad articulos*.

That "the knowledge of faith presupposes natural knowledge" which one can arrive at even without being a Christian is only one particular aspect of a much broader conception which in Christendom was accepted as a matter of course: namely, the notion of grace, which not only does not cancel out nature, let alone destroy it, but indeed needs it as a foundation. The famous sentence *gratia supponit naturam* means precisely that any "supernatural," divine gifts man may receive necessarily presuppose what man already possesses by virtue of his creation (one can also say: "by nature")— whether this supernatural gift takes the form of doctrine, or directive, or sacrament.

This brings us back to the theme *praeambula sacramenti*, by which are meant the presuppositions that man can, of himself, fulfill, and must have fulfilled, if an understanding and meaningful execution of the sacrament is to be expected. —In what follows we shall be dealing, above all, with these presuppositions, the *praeambula sacramenti*, which, by the way, cannot be adequately enumerated. Here we are discussing the core of Christian existence. This will be obvious to anyone who accepts that the Church itself is an essentially sacramental reality, in which the ultimate sacrament— God becoming man in Christ—remains present to us and is lived out.

Now if it is of the essence of sacrament to belong to the realm of signs (*sacramentum ponitur in genere signi:* with this sentence Thomas Aquinas indicates the direction to be taken in his tract about the sacraments in his *Summa theologiae*) it would follow that access to this sacramental living core of the Church would be impossible to anyone who simply did not understand what is involved in a sign.—I am speaking here firstly in the conditional tense. For one would expect that everyone would be familiar with such knowledge. It is a quite elementary thing which does not require any particular talent or education. Perhaps one could say that, on the contrary, a person who is educated, has done further studies, and reached a higher level of abstract, conceptual, and critical consciousness possibly has more difficulty in understanding—not what a sign "is," but what "it is for."

"Sign": if we consider the concept in a general way it means all that can be grasped by the senses—what we can see, hear, smell, taste, and touch—by which we are referred to something else which is not directly, if at all, available to these senses. As is immediately obvious, the world of signs contains an immeasurable multiplicity of phenomena. Rising smoke indicates the fact that there is fire and the place where it is; the tracks of deer in the snow; blushing as an indication of embarrassment; the white flag of capitulation; the wedding ring on the hand of a man and a woman—all of these are signs. But this completely random series already reveals an important demarcation line and with it a certain intrinsic complication. *All* signs have something in common: namely, that they point the person who sees them and seeks to interpret them to something different from the sign itself. But not all signs, but only some particular ones, go back to someone who wants to *say* something with the signs, i.e. *wants* to point to something different from the sign itself. In such a case, at least one person, a partner, is included—of whom it is expected that he can understand what is "said" by such signs and interpret the reference included in the signs. Of course, what one has in view are first and foremost the actions and gestures which express agreement or negation, rejection, or doubt. But I think communication through language is of greater importance here—the *word*, in which, in a unique and complete way the concept of sign is realized: because nothing that is knowable by the senses, i.e., audible to the listener, visible to the reader can point *so* clearly to something else as words can. —And if by symbol (and here there is a very broad spectrum of differing language usages, and yet a certain unity) one means that particular kind of sign in which something supra-sensory, something spiritual—perhaps also something holy—is presented *as itself*, and perhaps only meant for the initiated belonging to a community of believers, I would again say that there is no more perfect symbol than the *word*. Here we are thinking above all of words which name: names which Aristotle has already referred to as "symbols of things." I am speaking explicitly about words because this is what here, amongst artists, needs to be considered. This should not be forgotten when, in what now follows, as is right and normal, we seek to understand as the "language of faith" precisely the signs and symbols which are non-verbal. Besides, we want to retain here the distinction between sign and symbol even though the line separating them cannot easily be drawn with clarity. When the bell rings for Mass, that is a sign; but when the same bell rings for the "Angelus" it is a symbol.

However, mere knowledge of all of this does not mean that we pass through the courtyard of the sacraments; with such knowledge it is possible to *remain* in the courtyard—i.e., "outside." It is possible to have a differentiated grasp of what a sign is and of what a symbol is without so much as touching the threshold of the temple.

At the beginning, without expressly stating it, I quoted Thomas Aquinas—where he says that knowledge of faith presupposes natural knowledge. But Thomas has formulated this thought also in other more complete and more exact versions: "Faith presupposes natural knowledge just as grace presupposes nature, and completion presupposes that which is to be completed." This means what man has from birth and nature is designed for completion—completion through faith and sacrament. And only on the basis of such capacity for completion is it at all meaningful to speak of *praeambula* and "courtyards"—whether they be courtyards of faith or of sacrament. A priest friend of mine from the U.S., in his somewhat robust and uninhibited American way once gave the following translation for the sentence *gratia supponit naturam*: "You cannot baptize a baby unless you have a baby." Of course, that is both true and witty. However, I said to him: "But that is not the whole truth. The baby doesn't do it by itself, either." That means that as a Christian you only have the correct understanding of the "natural" if you see it as capable of completion and as something to be completed.

And with regard to natural *knowledge*, the received wisdom is valid: namely, that a truth which is merely known is not automatically part of my real life; I need to *want* it to be true. John Henry Newman made the distinction between notional knowledge and real knowledge, i.e., between abstract conceptual knowledge and real living knowledge. For example, everyone knows that a dying person at some point breathes his last breath; but only when someone is physically present at the death of a loved one does he know what it *really* means to draw one's last breath. Thus we can say: only someone who has taken his abstract knowledge of sign and symbol, also of "holy signs," into the middle of his existence and has in this way, as Newman says, "realized" it, can grasp the "symbolic or sacramental meaning." That is a phrase which, surprisingly enough, comes from Goethe. And it is worthwhile considering for a moment the context in which Goethe used this formulation. I must say I have always found it strange how seldom this has been referred to. The context, in which, by the way, there is also mention of "moral sensuality," cannot be otherwise described than as theology, or, more accurately, as controversial theology. In the seventh book of "Poetry and Truth (Dichtung und Wahrheit)—in the middle of his autobiography—where he is giving a concrete and intimate account of his very personal experiences, Goethe complains about the starkness of Protestant religious services; they are lacking in fullness. Then he says in conclusion: "Protestants have too few sacraments." And then the notion of sacrament is very carefully defined, naturally in his way, but the definition is worthy of consideration. It is described as "a sacred, august action which occurs at a point in reality which man cannot attain nor do without." And then follows a description of the seven sacraments which leaves nothing out and is fired with almost hymnic affirmation, and in which even the most orthodox Church censor would not easily discover a single false note—although the sequence Goethe follows is somewhat unusual: namely, he begins with marriage and ends with holy orders. And besides, he is quite clear in seeing holy orders as *consecratio* and not, for example, as appointment by the Church community. And this whole pages-long passage which I am concerned with here and from which I have already quoted the decisive words is prefaced by the sentence: "No Christian can experience it (the sacrament) with real joy if the sense for symbol and sacrament is not nourished in him." Quite clearly, therefore, Goethe sees here an indispensable precondition and presupposition; he sees here, as we can also express it, one of the *praeambula sacramenti*—and quite rightly.

But here the worrying question arises from which all of the above discussion originated: What could and must be done to nourish in people of our time the "sense for symbol and sacrament" invoked by Goethe? Are they in danger of losing it altogether? Has that happened already to a large extent? What can be done about it?

I would say that we would first of all have to begin by drawing attention to the "vacuum," the gap, the lack. Nothing at all will change without the insight that "something is wrong." But the fact that something is really fundamentally wrong can, I am convinced, be made clear to anyone who wants to listen. If it were simply impossible we would have to accept Jean-Paul Sartre's absurd thesis that there is no such thing as human nature (*il n'y a pas de nature humaine*), i.e., we would have to deny that man originates from a divine design and will, and is therefore ultimately an indestructible creature.

Of course, in trying to draw attention to the "vacuum" we should perhaps not begin immediately to speak about sacraments and also not formally speak about *praeambula sacramenti*—although that is exactly what we are concerned with. But we must presuppose that knowledge and acceptance of things such as "sacred signs" and pious symbols is at least feasible.

But it is best, as ever, to begin with a completely concrete situation. Take the average man, formed by the spirit of our times, fairly intelligent, alert, not dull, not without soul—this average man is waiting for his bus after work and after doing some quick shopping in the middle of a busy city. While he is standing there quietly, the bells of the "Angelus" begin to ring. This is nothing new to him. At the same time he begins to ponder a little, and suddenly a song he once knew comes to mind: "When the bells ring inviting rest, no one knows what they mean." He knows quite well *that* they mean something—and, indeed, not something directly practical (like the siren of an ambulance that you hear coming from a side street). Besides, our man has just taken a shortcut through a church in the market place. This may at first seem a somewhat improbable and artificial construct, but in reality that is, where I lived, quite normal. Many people do it. And so: he went through the church, naturally not to pray but also not disrespectfully and not without paying some attention. And as he went, he noticed with repeated surprise the innumerable burning candles obviously lit by people like himself. And these burning wax candles also come to mind as the sound of the bells from the tower of the same church cuts through the noise of the street.—What does he think about all of that? What does he make of it?

If he were to be asked about it openly his immediate answer would probably be: "I'm glad about all those things: bells, lights and other things of that kind. The world is barren and grey enough, and I am in favor of keeping this innocent brightness of our traditional customs, even if they are nothing more than memories." A hint of resignation in these last words is quite unmistakable. And, in fact, such an answer only seems to be positive. But we come across it in various forms all over the world. In India I very quickly learned that naturally women and girls, even stewardesses in airplanes, still bore on the forehead the red *tilaka*, the almond-sized red sign of Hindu temple piety, but that in the average case it was no longer a religious but rather a cosmetic symbol—which means no symbol at all. —It is true that the world must become a wilderness without order the more signs and symbols disappear from it. But to want to retain signs and symbols purely for their charm and color is a hopeless undertaking—for no other reason than that relegating them to the realm of aesthetics and the museums has destroyed the reality of signs. At the same time—and this is the worst part—it is made easy for us not to notice this loss of reality. We do "value" all this and could not do without it. And modern technology has enough possibilities to hand, in the form of perfect surrogates, to deceive us about such a loss.

In Washington Square in New York, where I was a guest of my publisher Kurt Wolff, I was awakened one morning by the sound of bells; I couldn't believe it. I remembered vaguely that on the previous evening I had seen a nearby church, a church tower. Then, when over breakfast I expressed my surprise about it, my host asked with unveiled irony: "What sort of bell-ringing did you hear: Notre Dame de Paris or was it St. Peter's in Rome?" In short: the church had no bells. There was only a record-player, probably in the parish office, and a loudspeaker in the tower. This is no laughing matter, for here we are confronted with a set of problems which are of serious concern to all of us and which are central to our present theme: the reality or unreality of signs and symbols. It is part of this reality that, on the one hand, there is someone who gives a discernible visual or audible sign; on the other hand, the person who discerns the sign is referred to a reality which may or may not be visible or audible. To conceal this clear state of affairs

and consign it to oblivion an unlimited number of technical possibilities is available. A broad area. I don't dare set foot in it. But
I would like to name one extreme example: I own an American
record on which an electronic well-tempered synthesizer produces
the impression of human song, and indeed—disturbingly—of the
beginning of Monteverdi's Vespers for the Blessed Virgin (*Deus,
in adjutorium meum intende*) intoned in Gregorian chant. It sounds
like song, like a symbolic act of quite special dignity; but in fact
there isn't anyone who sings! All that is left is the lovely veneer
("schöner Schein) which, however, is no longer lovely.

But let us return to our man who is waiting for his bus and let
us ask him now for his opinion about the reality of these signs. All
right, he says, there are, for example, the burning wax candles in
the church with which people want to express their reverence, adoration, gratitude. If they really feel all of that—is that not all that
counts, the inner sentiment? If this is genuine, where is the need
for candles? They don't add one iota. But if the sentiment is not
genuine the lit candle is a sign for something which does not exist!
And he would say that the same is true for all the "sacred signs"—
bells ringing, making the sign of the cross, genuflection, incense.
The only real thing about these signs is a material process to be
described using categories drawn from mechanics or chemistry.
The "flame consuming itself in warmth and light" of which Guardini speaks is in reality nothing but a chemical process of burning.
And what has this chemical process to do with reverence, dedication, adoration or gratitude?

This view can quite rightly be seen as representative of the
way people think in this day and age. Similarly, there is an emp-
tying out of reality from signs and symbols: both through a purely
aesthetical or aestheticist stance and through the spiritualistic and
materialistic splitting up of the world into two separate spheres,
so that there is only the spiritual or the material. With regard to
this separation, which Descartes introduced into European

thinking, of the *res cogitans*—of spiritual things—and *res extensa*—
of material things in the world of extension, it is impossible to
achieve clarity unless we go down to a deeper level of discussion.
Of course, it is not reasonable to dispute that the inner feeling in
the heart is crucial, whereas the candle and the incense are not.
And one cannot argue that a chemical process has, of itself, anything to do with adoration. Yet all of that immediately looks quite
different as soon as we have become clear about the fact that man
is "a built structure," or, more precisely, that man is both spiritual
and physical *at the same time*—so much so that there can be nothing
in man that is "purely spiritual" and nothing that is "purely material." Day by day, this fact is confirmed ever anew by the empirical
research of anthropologists: it is an idea with many implications.
It means not only that man is by his nature (as creature) a physical
being but also that the soul—as the living principle giving form to
the body from within—is itself in a certain sense physical. My
revered teacher and master, Thomas Aquinas, raises the following
objection to his own thinking—an objection which seems to have
exalted spiritual provenance. This is the objection: God is pure
spirit, and so the soul separated from the body must be more like
God than the soul bound up with the body! Against this, Thomas
says with great decisiveness: the soul bound up with the body is
more like God than the soul separated from the body because the
former is more perfectly in possession of its nature. "*Anima forma
corporis*: the soul is the *form* that gives shape to the body and the
body is that which is formed by the soul—moreover, this principle
formulated by the Church itself as binding doctrine (at the Council
of Vienna, 1321) is rightly referred to by Romano Guardini as the
foundation of all liturgical culture; this means that it is the foundation of our entire understanding of *those* sacred signs, the totality
of which constitute Christian worship. Man is not made in such a
way that any feeling he entertains can remain completely internal;
it must find expression; he must show it physically—in his facial

expression, by a gesture, by laughing, by an audible sound and, of course, in words. Clothing can express a joyous celebration or also mourning. But not only that! Man is also able to turn things from the external world into vocabulary for his language and gesture and to use them for communication. This applies not only to the flute and the organ—which we characteristically call "instruments"—but also to bells and candles as well as to all the works of sculpture and architecture which make wood, stone, and metal talk to us, i.e., make them into forms of human speech. Naturally, these all remain at the same time material things; they are measurable, they can be weighed, they can be understood in terms of mechanics and chemical analysis. And yet anyone who ignores—does not see, or does not want to see—the *non*-material aspect in the sound of bells, in the sign of the cross, in the wax candles on the altar and in all the other innumerable signs and symbols, has really understood nothing about them; as little, in fact, as someone who would see the speech of a living person as an exclusively phonetic and acoustic physiological process, or the written word as a quantum of printer's ink or graphite put down on paper in certain geometric shapes.

And yet the physicality and with it the materiality of the signs and symbols takes on a still greater importance and a quite new meaning when one considers that the signs, in order to make us aware of a spiritual reality that is not of the senses, have to be taken up and integrated into the life of our body—almost physiologically. In a simpler formulation: we have to know the sights and symbols "by heart"; only in this way, as Hegel once said, can their appropriation be "accomplished." Only when we know something by heart do we really know it. It is then known with the heart. And even the most intellectual/spiritual of the signs—the word—will only become completely ours through incorporation into the nerve pathways of our body's processes: through entrance into "the body's memory." Naturally this has to be preceded by strenuous intellectual learning by which what is known by heart is then is inscribed into the organs of the body (as an "engram," as the psychologists say); and it is, on the other hand, quite true that something learned by heart in such a way can also be reproduced and recited without engaging the mind—routinely, purely externally, and without any participation of the soul and the consciousness. But the reverse side of this is much more important: namely, that through this body memory something perhaps indispensable is in fact "retained," as we say. It is not lost even if reflective consciousness, the mind, knows nothing about it anymore, seems not to know about it, and even does not *want* to know about it anymore.

When the consciousness of a companion of Alexander Solzhenitsyn, delivered into the hut of a penal camp suffering from dysentery, had narrowed down to a tiny cell, this dying man meditated all day aloud on the Our Father and so remained near to the source of life. The wording of this incomparable prayer had to be *available* to him as something he knew by heart from childhood and could recite at any time, and something also recited a hundred times in the life of this man—without any engagement of the mind, mechanically, and as a matter of routine. —How often in life has a person who has been raised a Catholic made the sign of the cross without thinking! It is now so much part of his flesh and blood, as we say, that only this can possibly explain what happens at the death of Lord Marchmain, as Evelyn Waugh describes it in his novel "Brideshead Revisited." Old Lord Marchmain has returned to his ancestral house to die—after leading a dissolute life. He refuses the visit of the parish priest; he wants nothing to do with the last sacraments. But then, after his life has been draining away for a long time and the dying man seems to be no longer aware of anything, the priest, a truly spiritual man, is called and celebrates the sacrament of the final anointing. Then something quite unexpected happens. The narrator, who is in fact the main character in the novel, describes it as follows: "Suddenly Lord Marchmain raised his hand to his forehead. I thought he must have felt the touch of the chrism and was wiping it away. But the hand moved slowly down to his chest, then to his shoulder, and Lord Marchmain made the sign of the cross." What conceptual reflection cannot do and the mouth cannot speak is achieved by the hand in its symbolic gesture, expressing in signs, as is its nature, something which cannot be grasped by the senses. It brings this something not only to the mind of the dying man but also to someone else: namely, the narrator, who had also become an unbeliever and who now says about himself: "And a phrase came back to me from my childhood of the veil of the temple being rent from top to bottom." Naturally there would have been *nothing* there that could have been recalled by this symbolic gesture if the hand of this old man had not been trained from the beginning, and in early childhood had not been led and "informed" (in the double sense of the word!) by faith and understanding continually to make this sign of the cross.

This is now the point to speak of the infinite impoverishment which, in our contemporary civilized society, threatens the whole sphere of physical signs. We only need to think of the wretched level to which the words and gestures we use for greeting and speaking to people have been reduced. But also amongst Christians the number of sacred signs known by heart—naturally, including verbal symbols—has been narrowed down to the point where their very existence is threatened. We only need to compare normal usage today with what Romano Guardini immediately after World War I found it necessary to remind us in his little book "About Sacred Signs": the prayerful way the hands are held, genuflecting, bowing, beating the breast, "processing." Perhaps it is utopian to hope that the multiplicity of signs, which Guardini even back then recalled to mind as being almost consigned to oblivion, could be passed on to our young generation—at least making it plausible that one approaches Holy Communion in a different manner from the way in which one goes to the counter in the bank or a table in the restaurant.

Exactness and clarity are important for the function of a sacred sign—in the same way as we take it for granted with language of gesture amongst people. At the words of consecration spoken by the priest *in persona Christi* the rite of the Mass requires, as we know, that the celebrant, in speaking the words "He took the bread and gave thanks," really take the host in his hands. Now a young priest who quite intentionally did *not* move his hand at this moment answered my critical question saying that it made no difference if it happened five seconds later when the host was elevated. I then asked him what he would think if he offered someone his hand in greeting and the person left his hand in his pocket for five seconds.

I was embarrassed myself when a Greek Orthodox priest, an American, once showed me the shape of hand used in the Melkite Church for the sign of the cross: thumb, forefinger and middle finger together and the two other fingers below them: symbol of the Trinity, symbol of two natures in Christ! The two fundamental mysteries of faith—the Trinity and the Incarnation—represented by a sign in one single gesture!

As a twelve-year-old child I was taught by an old sacristan in our village how to ring the *Angelus* bell. First, these three heavy strokes: the supra-historical, so to speak heavenly enactment of the history of the Incarnation; and then come exactly thirty-three strokes as signs for the years of the life of Jesus on earth. Even today when I hear the *Angelus* I involuntarily begin to count; and then I notice that there are only more or less thirty-three strokes; perhaps it does not matter much. Still, exactness is a part of symbol.

Furthermore, today the subject of "ringing" necessarily brings another question to mind; and this question, too, is relevant to our subject "sign and symbol." Could we not do without bell-ringing?

Do our churches really need a tower? Let us pass over the embarrassing pronouncement of the German professor that this is all superfluous now that most people have a wristwatch. Here he has simply failed to recognize the symbolic meaning of the sounding of the bells. But, to come back to our question: *no* symbol is "necessary" for satisfying our basic needs; bells, candles, liturgical vestments are not necessary. It is of the nature of symbols to be "superfluous" and "exuberant" in the sense that they have *no* "useful" function. The same is true of signs—as in music and poetry—which are not "sacred" signs in the strict sense.

It is naturally a legitimate question whether the money for a bell would not be better spent on something to meet daily needs. And I will be careful not to criticize someone who, thinking of the misery in the world, insists that one's daily bread is more important the sound of bells. But there are various things to consider here. In St. John's Gospel, one of the apostles—Judas, by the way—says that it would be better to sell the precious ointment to help the poor. He receives the magisterial answer that it is more meaningful, through the needless spreading of a rich aroma, to bear witness to and to celebrate the divine presence in its complete elevation above daily life.—It also seems to me worth considering that, interestingly, the poor understand this far better than the replete. There is a story told by Pope Paul VI; his friend Jean Guitton, historian of philosophy at the Sorbonne, wrote it down and published it. As Archbishop of Milan, Montini, later to be Pope, one day visits a poor mountain village; the people receive him shyly and very cautiously. But they soon strike up a conversation, and the Bishop asks what it is they need most; he would like, if possible, to get it for them. "We need a baking oven." "Good. You will have it. I'll send you the money for it." After some time he inquired what happened about the oven. He was then told: we decided differently. During the war the church bell had been taken away from the village, and we preferred to use the money for a new bell. —The bell was, of course, not "necessary," but clearly indispensable!

Now, our theme is: "Sign and symbol as the language of Christian faith." But language is not just something spoken, but also something one hears and understands; and also the person who hears and understands, even if, perhaps, he himself is not at all able to speak, participates in language through understanding and hearing. Up to now we have spoken almost exclusively about the first aspect: namely, signs, through which we "say" something. But now we have to speak of those signs which we do not ourselves give, but which rather are given to us and through which God "says" something to us. Such signs given to us by God are above all the *sacraments*. They are called, and also in a much stricter sense are, the language of Christian faith—not the language spoken by us, but the divine language which the Christian has to hear and understand. This duty is expected of him and entrusted to him. Naturally, anyone who ignores (from an aesthetic, spiritualist, or materialist standpoint) the reality of the signs, especially the "sacred" signs made by man, or, in other words, does not engage with these *praeambula sacramenti*, will understandably not have the presuppositions for understanding the sacraments themselves. No one who has become deaf to the language of signs and symbols can understand these really creative signs which not only, like the signs we create ourselves, *mean* something but also at the same time *effect* what they *mean*.

This claim will certainly seem, to any kind of rationalism which claims it has a supposedly scientific base, to be a "magical" or "mythical" or "archaic" residue of a primitive, pre-scientific view of the world. The expression "supposedly scientific" emanates from Karl Jaspers, who, in his debate with Rudolf Bultmann, says that such science is nothing but the "average enlightenment of all ages." And indeed it seems to me that Bultmann's demythologization thesis—which exerts wide influence on the theology of our age— serves as a model case of the radical tendency to empty the sacraments of their real meaning. And it is quite logical that, for Bultmann, first on the long list of the notions which are supposedly done away with because they are "mythical" is the fundamental sacrament: the Incarnation of the divine Logos. One can see the superior attitude of astonishment, the shaking of the head, as this central message of Christianity is given the formulation: "A pre-existent divine being appears on earth as a human being!" And naturally the greatest of the seven sacraments is not missing from the list, because surely no modern man, whether he thinks in bio-logical or idealistic terms, could possibly understand that "a meal could give him spiritual strength." But Bultmann is, as I have said, only a model case. The mind that thinks exclusively in abstract concepts always feels tempted to judge the compact concretization of the invisible-divine to be only too "material." This temptation is also found where a modern Catholic theologian says that the essence of sacrament lies in the word (by which he means, in this context, something *quite different* from sign and symbol). Even Au-gustine seems to be warding off a dangerous threat when he vig-orously insists that in the Eucharist we are not concerned with mere words ("not language, not written characters, not word sounds ...") but with the body of the Lord incorporated in the real symbol of material formed from the fruits of the earth.

I do not intend—and it would not be within my competence—to speak more in detail about the theology of the sacraments. I would like to remain in the territory of the *praeambula sacramenti*, in the courtyard of theology, although it is an area where, indeed, not a little is decided. To me it seems highly significant, for exam-ple, that it is a philosopher, Karl Jaspers (with whom, naturally, I do not always agree in other things) who corrects the theologian Bultmann and accuses him of a shallow enlightenment approach. It is precisely the sphere of nature that is under discussion here. And I am happy, in conclusion, to make the point again that pre-cisely Goethe, such an open "man of the world," called the sense for symbols also the "sacramental sense"—which ultimately means that only a person in which this "symbolic or sacramental sense" is "nourished" can experience and receive what God has had in mind for him: an invisible-divine gift in earthly form.

"Thinking has its beginnings in image, as in an unconscious state" (Konrad Weiss).—Image is prior to word, and prior to the firmly defined thought is the sensuous, the so-to-speak less spiritual image. Before the son is Maria. But the word comes from the image; and a word separated from the image is unfruitful. And this relationship, like that between the root and the green plant, is real although the image is the blinder and word is the more seeing element; although word intrinsically is of higher rank, so that it takes its origin from the image as if from an unconscious state. Word separated from this origin and seeking to find its contentment in this self-sufficient "Intellectuality" cheats itself of its own fruit: as long as Orpheus proceeds blindly, Eurydice follows him; but as soon as he— only too confident of success (or: losing faith, which is always something blind)—wants to see with his own independent faculties, his spouse returns to the region of the dead; through his desire to see, he destroys the work that began in blindness. But thought and word must retain in its purity the link with the image, which is relatively blind; without the image, thought and word have no historical effectiveness. It is not the "idea" of bravery, but the image, the symbol (lion, eagle, banner) that has a direct effect; not the conceptually formulated idea of love, but the image of the pelican nourishing its young with its own blood. The Word, the Logos of God, becomes effective in history by being born "of Mary," becoming a visible person; and Mary, although less powerful than her offspring, remains the mediatrix. (1943)

Before their meal, the Greeks used to make an offering of wine to the gods from a goblet. What striking form is there now in which a modern person could express the same reverence, gratitude, expiation, desire for reconciliation? (1942)

Knowledge and Freedom

The formulation "Science and Freedom," in today's context, is aimed at an antagonistic point of view. It is aimed at an opponent who theoretically denies the freedom of science as well as consciously endangers, limits, and destroys it.

But when this antagonism involves an intellectual debate and not a mere "demonstration" (the dramatic change in meaning of this word "demonstration" has a hidden relevance to the theme!), it is then necessary that the opposite position be known not only in the form of its concrete manifestation, but in its roots. Only then can clarity be expected about the kind and strength of argument that would be a sufficient counter to the intrinsic thrust of the opponent's view. Of course, it could also come about that, for the sake of refuting the opponent one would suddenly see the need to review one's own presuppositions. Anyone who undertakes to investigate the way the totalitarian state presses science into its service will, in fact, have this kind of experience. More precisely: anyone who resists such pressure which impinges on the freedom of science—anyone who responds, not by way of political struggle and active or passive resistance but by way of *intellectual debate* (this alone concerns us here), will see himself confronted with arguments which he cannot refute without correcting some notions which in Western civilization have been taken for granted for centuries. These are notions which contradict that which, still earlier, was considered valid beyond doubt; i.e., they contradict what not only the great teachers of Christendom thought—Augustine as well as Thomas—but also Plato and Aristotle. These old and those new notions are precisely relevant to our theme: namely, the meaning of knowledge as such and the link between knowledge and freedom.

What I would like to propose, positively, is the following: to counter the decline in scientific freedom as it is found in the totalitarian worker state, an effective argument can only be found, in the sphere of intellectual debate, if at the same time some fundamental insights are brought into play which were formulated in the pre-modern Western tradition.

We must now speak of these insights, if only in a somewhat summary form. One of them—the most important one—is expressed in Aristotle's Metaphysics. On the first pages of this book, which may be described as one of the "canonic" works produced by the Western mind, freedom of knowledge is mentioned. But, to be more precise: it is said of a *particular* kind of knowledge, of a particular endeavor to know that it is, amongst all branches of knowledge, free in the highest degree; and that this is "obviously" the case. What is meant is knowledge concerned with the whole of reality, with the structure of the world as a whole. What is meant is consideration of the question: what, ultimately and fundamentally, is the essence and the being of things? This refers to the application of our knowing faculties—driven by the force of our innermost spirit—to seek their full and undiminished object, which has no limits. What is meant is "knowledge as such," which does not remain limited to anything particular but takes in all individual acts of knowledge which have as their object a particular aspect of reality, including "scientific" knowledge. To put it briefly, what is meant here is the type of knowledge which Aristotle refers to as the "most really *philosophical*." It becomes clear that it is not a question of something apart—as "metaphysical" (Aristotle did not use the term, nor did he know of it). Instead, it is a question of the impetus of our knowing power as a whole, which is at work precisely *in* all concrete experiences and in the conclusions we draw, gathering and including them all as it seeks out the object appropriate to it: the whole. This kind of knowledge is what Aristotle says is the only free kind.

The question is: what does "free" mean here? We are touching here the critical, neuralgic point of the problem. "Free" according to Aristotle (and here he is formulating what is probably an entirely ancient idea, which was used, for example, by his teacher, Plato, and which later exerted a commanding influence on the whole of Western thought)—"free" means as much as "non-practical." Praxis means the achieving of aims; that which *serves* to achieve an end is "the practical." But the kind of knowledge which deals with the ultimate foundation of the world is alone supposed not to "serve" a purpose (that is the general opinion); it is (supposedly) not even possible or thinkable to put it to any use: "it alone is there for its own sake." Now exactly this not being there for anything else, but for itself and for its own sake—this is what human language sees as "freedom."

But in this unbelievably concise paragraph of a little more than twenty lines in Aristotle's Metaphysics some further characteristics of that free and non-practical knowledge are added and should not be omitted. Aristotle adds the following: the knowledge that focuses on the totality of the world, purely for the sake of knowing and to that extent free—this knowledge cannot possibly be achieved by man; he never fully grasps it; it is therefore not something that man has without limitation, since, as a human being he is himself subject to many kinds of necessities, to serve. One would have to say that only God can achieve this knowledge completely, just as it is also the divine root of all things to which this knowledge aspires. For this very reason no other kind of knowledge has the rank and dignity of philosophical knowledge, although they are all more necessary: *necessariores omnes, dignior nulla* (as the Latin version of the ancient Greek puts it). So much for Aristotle.

That is the sketch of a world view in which the concept of "scientific freedom" has its origin. But with "origin" we are not merely referring to the historical source, although this, too, has to be considered, for it is indeed the case that in the second chapter of Aristotle's Metaphysics the two concepts of "freedom" and "knowledge" are considered in relationship to one another in the history of Western thought. A thousand and a half years later Thomas Aquinas, in his commentary on this same chapter, formulated the definition of the *artes liberales* (from this term the medieval name of the philosophical faculty—Arts Faculty—derives its name). And if, exactly one hundred years ago, John Henry Newman, in his book which has since become a classic, "*The Idea of a University*," speaks of "liberal knowledge or a gentleman's knowledge," he is explicitly placing himself in the same tradition.

But more important than the historical derivation seems to me to be the fact that the concept of, or rather the claim for "scientific freedom" has to lose its legitimation and its inner credibility when it becomes separated from its origin: namely, from the foundation of that world view. This is, I believe, what has happened at the beginning of the modern age.

The fundamental world view, which is, of course, more a view of the essence of man and the meaning of his existence, can be expressed briefly as follows: *First*: however much man is a practical being who needs to use the things of the world to meet his requirements for living, he does not acquire his real riches through technical subordination of the forces of nature but through the purely theoretical knowledge of reality. The existence of man is all the richer the more deeply he has access to reality and the more it is opened up to him. Through his knowledge he achieves the purest realization of his being, so that even his ultimate perfection and fulfilment consist in knowledge; Eternal Life is called a *visio*. — This is not a notion derived specifically from Christian theology. It is found also in Aristotle. Anaxagoras expresses it in his own way when, in answer to the question "why were you born?" he says: "To look at the sun, the moon, and the sky"—by which he would not have meant the physical heavenly bodies but the construction of the world as a whole.

Second: because man, in his theoretical knowledge is doing – more than in any other way—that which he fundamentally and really wants to do (and this is what the concept of "freedom" really consists in: doing what one wants to do!), not only is his "knowledge" to be termed "free," and all the more so the more it is theoretical; but also *man himself* is freer, the more his knowing is theoretical, directed to truth and nothing else. This accords with experience: anywhere that a person, independently of looking after life's immediate goals, approaches reality purely as a knower; wherever, without being worried about usefulness, damage, danger, death, he is able to see and to say: "That is how it is and not otherwise" ("The Emperor has no clothes on")—in these circumstances human freedom is realized in a special sense. Truth makes you free, as the venerable saying has it.

In the West, this has been re-formulated again and again. Martin Heidegger is also speaking from within the same tradition when he situates the essence of truth in freedom.

Three: There are levels of knowledge—and therefore also of the freedom realized in knowing. The highest level would be attained if our knowing faculties grasped their object completely; in this case the most extreme level of freedom would be realized; man would be doing, in the most perfect way, what he really wants. But I am using a hypothetical subjunctive. This goal *cannot* be achieved by man in his bodily existence in history, although it is what keeps the whole thrust of this same existence in motion. That is Aristotle's meaning where he says: the question about the foundation of reality as a whole "is one which always and ever, and today, is posed—a continually open question." The medieval commentator, Thomas Aquinas, made this profound remark about the statement: precisely because the answer cannot be at our disposal as our own, this wisdom is sought after for its own sake (included here is the statement that we cannot seek the answers as ultimate answers once and for all—as they are to be found in the exact sciences. Not in the full sense of "for their own sake," not as something meaningful in itself in the highest possible way.)

At this point something very incisive is being said, I believe, about *science* (in the narrower sense): despite the exactness of its answers it is not the highest form of knowledge. And also with regard to freedom it occupies a middle position, an almost ambiguous one. This is seen in two ways—*first point:* man's self-limitation to scientific knowledge in the strict sense can mean that he loses his openness for the unlimited object of knowledge. In other words: there is a particular form of intellectual un-freedom, the root of which is the exclusive ideal of science. *Second point:* it is not contrary to the nature of science to be used for purposes which are extrinsic to it. No injustice is done to science if it accepts tasks emanating from the sphere of praxis—whether this be political, economic, technical, or military. This does not destroy science; whereas philosophy, because it is concerned with the whole of reality, with the object of knowledge which is sought after simply for its own sake, would be *eo ipso* destroyed by such employments. One can think one is taking philosophy into service, but behold!— what is taken into service is no longer philosophy! Of course, there is also in science, at its inner core, an element which cannot be pressed into service: that is the philosophical element of *theoria*, which is geared to truth and nothing else. That means that science has, by its very nature, a claim to freedom to the extent that it is not practical, but theoretical.

This is the quintessence of all that we know so far: freedom of knowledge is closely bound up with—indeed, identical with—its theoretical character. Anyone who infringes on scientific freedom or destroys it can do this only by infringing on or destroying its theoretical character. On the other hand: anyone who surrenders the theoretical character of knowledge or declares it unessential by comparison with practicality is passing up the possibility of defending any claim to scientific freedom.

We are put in this strange position by some theses proposed at the beginning of the modern era which have become a constituent part of modern consciousness. We can admit that these theses came to light not without legitimate reasons, and yet we can still consider that they are false or at least in need of correction. I am thinking here of the sentence in Descartes's *Discours sur la méthode* that a new, "practical" philosophy needs to replace the old theoretical one in order to put us in a position to become masters and owners of nature (*par laquelle ... nous pourrions ... nous rendre comme maîtres et possesseurs de la nature*)—a thought which recurs almost word for word in the thesis of American pragmatism, that all human knowledge has the character of being a tool in the context of the "intellectual industry"; that "giving security to life and enjoyment of life is the aim of all intellectual activity"; that, above all, philosophy is ultimately not aimed at acquiring knowledge of the world but at finding ways to control it. I will quote a third thesis: "A scientist who is preoccupied with abstract problems should never forget that the aim of all science consists in satisfying the needs of society." No one will want to say that there is a difference, in principle, between the thesis represented by Descartes and Dewey on the one hand and, on the other hand, the last thesis I have quoted—taken, with some cunning!, from the Great Soviet Encyclopedia (Große Sowjet-Enzyklopädie).

In all of these theses the theoretical character of knowledge is openly denied. (Anyone, furthermore, who approaches reality exclusively with the attitude of "how do I become master and owner?" is simply not capable of focusing purely theoretically— i.e., being concerned with truth and nothing else—with the totality of the world and with the essence of things.) —But freedom has also become impossible; more accurately, it has become impossible to defend it with any credible argument.

If science in the totalitarian worker state finds itself in the situation where it continually has to answer the inquisitorial question: what is your contribution to the Five-Year-Plan?—this is nothing but a strictly drawn conclusion from Descartes' thesis about the philosophy of the *maître et possesseur de la nature*.

We see here an extreme possibility which no longer seems totally foreign to our experience. If we no longer have certainty that knowledge of truth is what makes the spirit free, it can perhaps come about that the concept of freedom itself is questionable and beyond the grasp of our minds: we don't know what it means. — Thus one reads with concern, in the last diaries of André Gide, the entry: "Thousands are prepared to sacrifice their lives to bring about a better standard in living conditions: more justice, a more equal sharing of earthly goods; I scarcely dare to add: more freedom—*because I don't know exactly what is meant by it.*" —But we can pass over the question of how this strange note is to be interpreted.

My only aim has been to make clear that the concept "scientific freedom" is rooted in rich soil, perhaps deeper than expected, and that a radical attack like the one we are dealing with at present causes its defenders to consider this origin.

There is an important sentence which, in a moving way, names this origin: the ultimate form of freedom of the knower. The sentence is significant above all because of the man and because of the particular situation in which he spoke it or, rather, wrote it down. The man is, in the most distinguished way, a Western figure: a Roman who did his studies in Athens and then, at the court of a Germanic prince, sought to communicate the wisdom inherited from antiquity to the new age that was looming: *Boethius*. But the situation is that of a prisoner. From his prison cell where he awaits execution, Boethius assures himself of his ultimate, indestructible freedom, saying: "The human soul is necessarily at its freest when it remains in contemplation of the divine spirit."

Freedom and Pornography

Our opinions, like our actions, usually come about in two different ways. We either have our "reasons" for them, or we come to them through some kind of psychological or physiological causality which is independent of our thinking. Perhaps both reasons and causes are always involved. And it may be that we sometimes believe or claim that we have a reason, whereas, in truth, causes are at work. Of course, this does not affect the validity of the distinction.

Reasons are derived from the facts, or, more accurately, from knowledge of the facts. It is not by chance that the term "Grund" (the German term being translated here) is *ratio* in Latin, *raison* in French, and *reason* in English. If a person predicts a bad end for a particular proposed undertaking because he knows the circumstances and the persons involved, he has a reason for his prediction. But if this pessimistic prognosis, as is quite conceivable, had to do with a tendency to see the worst because of a disorder of the gallbladder, a cause but not a reason would be involved.

The link with the theme "freedom" is clear enough. The more reasons a person has and the more strongly he is moved by them the more he is free. On the other hand, the more effective the causes, the greater is his lack of freedom and the greater his dependence—one could almost say: his enslavement. It is not that he has been "induced." He has been determined by something.

But what does all this have to do with pornography? —The calculation made by this large business enterprise obviously aims at starting a particular series of causal connections and producing a determining influence on the consumer. This means putting him again and again into a condition of at least temporary bondage. It does not need to work for more than an instant, as long as it is enough for the purchase of an entry ticket or a magazine. Curiously, people are regularly up in arms because they think that freedom is being threatened as soon as it appears that big business is being curtailed—where profit depends on nothing other than the reduction of freedom.

Philosophy and the Common Good

For the perfection of human society it is, according to the ancients, necessary that there are people dedicated to the *vita contemplativa*. Of any ten people who might read such a thing today probably eight would find this opinion incomprehensible or simply false; and hardly one would, even if he thought contemplative life was something quite meaningful and respectable, not want to call contemplation "necessary"—and certainly not "socially" necessary.

Besides: what would that opinion of the ancients have to do with the theme "Philosophy and the Common Good?" since clearly contemplation is not philosophy.

And yet the following thoughts are based on the conviction that the old proposition about the social necessity of the *vita contemplativa* is, first of all, strictly true, and is, secondly, entirely pertinent to our theme.

But there is clearly no sense in proceeding with the argument without saying what is meant by "the common good" and by "philosophy."

I open with Plato, the ancestor of all Western philosophy. Socrates says of the wise men of old and of himself that the philosophizer keeps his distance from matters concerning the state; the sophist, Protagoras, considers that the "philosophy" he teaches prepares one to be effective in the city state through public speaking and a life of activity (which means that Plato thought differently); the sophist's pupil, Callicles, says: a person who is preoccupied with philosophy after his early years fails to learn what is necessary to achieve power and honor in the city state (which again means, though not in the same sense, that Plato has a different opinion); and Socrates again: the real philosophizer usually does not even know where the Town Hall is, and around the courts he makes a quite laughable impression. If we then take into account that the two most voluminous works of the same Plato, which are philosophical works in the most profound sense—the "Republic" and "Laws"—and we see that they deal precisely with the political organization of the community, then we sense both the complexity of our problem and the need for clarity regarding the fundamental concepts.

So, what is meant by "common good" and "philosophy"? "Common good," *bonum commune*: that is the "good" which truly contributes to the well-being of human society and for which society exists. It crystallizes the values which a social organization— above all, that of the state—would have to realize if it could be said to fulfil the possibilities with which it is endowed. This is, of course, a purely formal and abstract designation. It only becomes interesting when we try to say what the concrete meaning of *bonum commune* is. It is then that we realize that it cannot be said exhaustively and definitively, for that would presuppose that we could say exhaustively and definitively what possibilities are to be found in human society and ultimately what it is. And it is not possible to say—no more than it is possible to say what the human person really and definitively is. For this reason no one can exhaustively say what, materially (*materialiter*) and concretely, is the "good" for which man exists and which he would have to realize in his life if it could be said of him that he has realized his possibilities (this is, after all, what is meant by Socrates when, in "Meno," he doggedly maintains that he does not know "what virtue is" and that he has not yet met anyone who does know). —But all of this does not mean that we can say nothing at all about the concrete content of the *bonum commune*. Rather, the point is that what is said cannot have a claim to being exhaustive and definitive.

At first sight this idea may well seem to be "purely academic." Yet the reality is that it has extremely political relevance.

It is an essential characteristic of every totalitarian regime that those who have political power claim to define, exhaustively and definitively, the concrete content of the *bonum commune*. The problematic aspect of the "Five Year Plan" is not the attempt to match production and demand. What is really disastrous is that the "Plan" becomes the exclusive criterion for the whole of life—for mining, for university curricula, for organization of the individual's leisure time, for the creative work of painters, writers and musicians—so that everything which does not meet the criterion is declared "socially unimportant" and "undesirable" if not forbidden, and is suppressed.

But there is another characteristic of contemporary social planning: the plans are, naturally, almost exclusively based on *usefulness*. That means that the concept of the "common good" is explicitly narrowed down to mean "common usefulness"—so that the claim to define *bonum commune* exhaustively and definitively says, in addition, that only what is useful contributes to the well-being of human society.

The disturbing thing is that that which happens in the modern totalitarian worker state—explicitly and in a radical form—is happening in the whole world, although not explicitly and less radically. It is disturbing that in the whole world this imperceptibly increasing identification of "common good" with "common usefulness" is taking place. This can be seen in, amongst other things, the fact that philosophy and philosophizing are considered more and more as a mere intellectual luxury, as something which is barely compatible with "social conscience"—a kind of sabotage of one's "really important" tasks. This step is not in the slightest surprising. It is, in fact, simply unavoidabl— if "common good" is the same as "common usefulness," for philosophy is defined precisely as not belonging to the sphere of usefulness. If, on the other hand, the ancients said philosophy was necessary ("necessary for the perfection of human society"), this was only possible because they understood that the concept "common good," while including "common usefulness," also included more—as the whole includes the part but is more.

This brings us back to our theme, the discussion of which, as we have seen, throws up fundamental questions.

But we still have to say more clearly what philosophy is. Is it really the same as contemplation (which up to this point seems to have been implicitly presupposed)? Yes, in some respects philosophy is contemplation. Cicero and Seneca used *contemplatio* as the Latin translation of the Greek *theoria*. And *theoria* is indeed the inner core of philosophy. But what is *theoria*? The ancients' answer was that *theoria* is an engagement with the world which aims at nothing but truth, an attitude of silent listening, distinct, above all, from the attitude of one actively realizing goals. Theoretical means precisely non-practical. But is there not also *theoria* in every genuine branch of knowledge, like physics or sociology? There is. But the realization of *theoria* is only "pure" in philosophizing. Every branch of knowledge is constituted by approaching reality with a definitely formulated question—which is why it is in this respect not silent. The philosophizer, on the other hand, who wants to know what all that is fundamentally about, what "reality" "really" means—one who seeks this kind of knowledge does not start out with a definitely formulated question in the way a scientist does. Precisely this attitude of wordless listening enables him, on the one hand, to see all information from every branch of knowledge as a contribution to the answer he is really looking for; on the other hand, it disposes him not to be satisfied with any of these items of information but to remain open to the ultimate "wisdom," aspiring to which is central to the concept of *philo-sophia*.

But is there not also such a thing as practical philosophy? No. The really philosophical form of philosophy, the philosophical doctrine of being—the "first philosophy" (as Aristotle meant it)—can certainly not be practical. "All knowledge that is wisdom and is called philosophy is knowledge for its own sake: it is therefore theoretical and not practical." This is what Aquinas says in his commentary to Aristotle's Metaphysics. All intellectual life, even all praxis, originates in the pure process of becoming conscious of reality, and the philosophical aspect of philosophy is precisely that it is the place where this process is nurtured.

This means two things: something negative and something positive.

—The negative: it is not possible to philosophize for the sake of realizing some sorts of goals. That is impossible by the very nature of the thing. The positive: in the purely theoretical, philosophizing engagement with reality man can achieve freedom which cannot be had elsewhere and in any other way, and in which even the fact of external lack of freedom can possibly be irrelevant. This is the reason why the ancients referred to the man devoted to *theoria* as "blissful" in a special sense. It is the inner freedom from looking after concrete needs, the satisfying of which is the function of praxis. (Naturally, in the long run man cannot exist in this way; but in the moments of *theoria* he succeeds again and again in transcending the sphere of the everyday.)

So here we have some essential elements of the concept of "philosophy."

At this point an objection is raised: when Descartes, in line with Bacon, demands a "practical philosophy" he is clearly formulating a different kind of philosophy which seems to overcome and cancel out the conflict (of philosophy) with the world of practical living as the ancients see it. Reply: if philosophizing means that man is preoccupied with the roots of things, the ultimate meaning of being, the real sense of "all of this," the Bacon/Descartes approach—the approach of the philosophy of the modern era—must indeed be understood as philosophy destroying itself. Anyone who thinks of reality as the raw material of human activity cannot even start to ask the question about the roots of things—the really philosophical question—no more than one can love a person other than for himself.

Another objection: is this separation and tearing apart of *theoria* and practice not meaningless?—Reply: if we insist on retaining the purity of *theoria*, i.e., of its indifference to praxis, we are thereby defending the fruitfulness of *theoria* and proclaiming the link between *theoria* and praxis.

As I already said: all praxis deserving of the name of "human activity" comes from the pure process of becoming aware of reality. This is the meaning of Goethe's words: "In our deeds and actions everything depends on the objects' being purely grasped and treated according to their nature." Praxis is based on an engagement with reality which aims at becoming aware of reality, i.e., of truth and nothing else. In other words: *theoria* is only fruitful for praxis as long as it is not concerned with *being* fruitful.

Seen in this way, there is also a certain indirect relationship— one that is certainly difficult to formulate—between philosophical *theoria* and "ordinary practicality." Naturally we still have to consider that the theoretical element in individual branches of knowledge, despite being a philosophical element, is nevertheless not real "philosophy."

But this still does not explain the full sense of the statement quoted at the beginning, according to which, philosophy is necessary for the perfection of human society. —To show this necessity and to give it a clearer formulation we need first of all to say what real philosophizing results in, to what insights it leads. Then it may be possible to say what philosophy "does" for the common good—the latter being understood, naturally, as distinct from "common usefulness."

I am trying to imagine the ironic look of puzzlement on Socrates' face if he were to have heard this question. But also

Aristotle, who with his systematic mind is rightly called the founder of a more "scientific" philosophy, says that it is of the nature of a philosophical question that it is brought closer to a solution but can never be answered once and for all. This is not to say that philosophizing despairs of meaning, but, on the contrary, that it is characterized by hope. Of course, hope also includes the negative element that *sophia*—the ultimate answer—cannot be already in our possession as belonging to us. And, in fact, which of the philosophical questions—What is the real? What is man? What is knowledge?—has found an answer to match the finality associated with the discovery that the TB bacillus is the cause of pulmonary consumption? According to Thomas Aquinas, the efforts of philosophers have not yet succeeded in fathoming the nature of a single gnat.

And so, what is philosophizing "good" for?

Is this not already something good for us to find, again and again, that being, the world, reality—which I cannot possibly give up pondering—is unfathomable? I am unable to get to the bottom of it. The more I know about things, the further the sphere of the not-yet-known stretches out in front of me as immeasurable. Do we perhaps not need precisely the fact that we are again and again prevented from forgetting that the world—including the self—is a mystery? Experiences of this kind certainly do not make us "capable"; they amount to us being "profoundly moved." But we are not properly human if we are not able to be profoundly moved by coming aware of the deeper aspect of the world. And so this would be the role of philosophy: to help man to experience again and again, along with the mysterious character of the world, his own unfinished state, the not-yet of his own being and existence—and this despite all the skill and fascinating perfection of scientific knowledge and achievement which continually seduces the "lord and owner of nature" into taking too shallow a view of himself and the world.

Are there, then, no objective philosophical outcomes, no insights which could be expressed in propositions? And how would the answer "no" be reconcilable with the classical teaching of the *philosophia perennis*? There are, in fact, objective philosophical insights which can be formulated in propositions. But they do not amount to a "system," and certainly not to a "closed system" which could lay claim to be an adequate reflection of the essential reality of the world. In the great tradition of Western philosophy, the objective outcome of philosophizing which can be formulated in propositions has always been considered "scant," although Thomas Aquinas says in his commentary on Aristotle's Metaphysics: the little knowledge that can be achieved in the "First Philosophy" is of more weight than all else that can be known in the sciences.

Experience of the mysterious character of reality is not a mere *negativum*, no more than is the "I know that I don't know" of Socrates; when it is a really knowing encounter and not a merely vague feeling this experience penetrates deeper and finds a "truer" truth about the world than any exact science can do. Only a discerning encounter with the mystery—which consists in the fact that something is—only this experience gives us the awareness that the light which makes things "positively" knowable, is simply unfathomable and inexhaustible and thus, at the same time, makes things incomprehensible. Science has to do with the positively knowable aspect of things; philosophy is formally concerned with the underlying incomprehensibility. Therefore philosophical knowledge, although it cannot be formulated in terms of a positive outcome or an "answer," is nevertheless the deeper truth.

What does philosophy contribute to the common good? —The answer will depend on our conception of what is "good" for man, for the individual as well as for the community, and on what is of real value to him. The opinion of the ancients (Plato, Aristotle, Augustine, Thomas) seems to me highly significant: that man's true and genuine advantage is not that he can satisfy his daily needs, not that he can be the lord and proprietor of nature and its forces. The "noblest form of possession," the most genuine way to conquer the world, is through knowledge of reality.

The more the world becomes accessible and opened up, the richer our existence. This applies not only to the individual but also to the community: society, too, lives from truth manifested "publicly" in a higher or lower degree. That does not mean, of course, that politics, as the endeavor to achieve the common good, is not first and foremost concerned with satisfying basic needs, with the preservation of external peace and the country's internal order, and with harnessing the forces of nature. But the ancients say: all of this is a necessary presupposition, but only a presupposition for man taking possession of the things that are of real value to him. And so philosophy is not merely a part of the common good, but because in philosophical *theoria*, in contemplation, and in it alone (not in science) the unfathomable, divine foundation of things is accessible and the mastery of reality in the highest sense takes place, the enabling of contemplation is the objective of politics: "It is"—as Thomas says in the Commentary on Aristotle's Nicomachean Ethics—"the joy of vision, *felicitas speculativa*, to which all political life seems to be oriented."

The inner division of all earthly power between Emperor and Pope ("the inner core is split, and knowledge and life are not the same," as Konrad Weiß says) so that neither can be replaced by the other and neither can do without the other—this division is, so to speak, the impoverished and deficient form of the concept bonum commune. *In the abstract it can be said that the meaning of political power is the realization of the* bonum commune. *But in historical fact the concept suffers from the split between the two elements.*

Contemporary Relevance
of the Cardinal Virtues:
Prudence, Justice, Courage, Moderation

We have to cope with the fact that, in the sphere of language, words are always going to suffer wear and tear. Precisely the "grand" words—or more accurately, the words which signify something ethically sublime, something human therefore, something required of man—are susceptible to such a decline; suddenly one does not want to hear them or utter them; they have become a scandal. Who has not, in paging through a magazine in the hairdresser's salon, not felt the dire need never again to speak the word "love"? As C. S. Lewis says, "Give a good thing a name and after some time it will be a name for a defect." In this sphere that seems to be the way of the world.

I said: we have to cope with the fact. The question is, how to do it. There is no recipe. We might be inclined to declare that a certain word is dead and to withdraw it from service. More than twenty years ago I quoted from Paul Valéry's speech before the Academy in which he said the word "virtue" is dead (since it was only being used in comic opera, in the catechism, and in the *Académie Française*). But words which are fundamental to human language cannot simply be made to disappear. And they can hardly be replaced by another word. What word, for instance, could be used to replace "love"? It is a difficult problem also in the case of the word "virtue." The attempt has been made, but the result has been something esoterically odd. An eminent Plato translator, Kurt

Hildebrandt, says for *areté* "capability" (Tüchtigkeit)—because the word "virtue" makes you think of a virtuous maiden. I'm not sure what seriously can be said against a "virtuous maiden," but "capability" is simply something quite different from what is meant by the word *areté* and virtue; the suggested replacement is quite simply wrong. It does not reflect Plato's meaning, but that of the sophists.

Then what is to be done? I have two suggestions. First: to be extremely sparing in the use of the great and therefore endangered words. Second: to look anew at the true, original meaning contained in and behind these words and to paraphrase them always with fresh expressions which are as little worn as possible and which everyone can understand. In this way, the original meaning can be kept alive in the general consciousness—for example, also the original, probably still valid meaning of the word "virtue." Perhaps then people will not think it important whether a word sounds "chic" and modern or outmoded; and perhaps one will be less inclined to "smile" on hearing or reading the word virtue (as Max Scheler notes and regrets in his famous essay on the rehabilitation of virtue [Zur Rehabilitation der Tugend] written during World War I).

This brings us to our theme. In answer to an aggressively precise question once formulated by Immanuel Kant, "What is being asked here?" one could say: we want to know whether the concept of virtue—and the understanding of the human criterion for behavior based on it—has any direct relevance to people living in our time. Or is the concept of virtue and the theory of virtue to be discarded? More drastically: can "virtue" be "saved" or not? At this point one of Plato's sayings, from the last chapter of the Republic, comes to mind. There, too, they are discussing whether a particular teaching, a message, some wise utterance (the subject is life after death) can be "saved" and thus be made accessible to people born in a later age; but Plato adds: it is much more important to hope that that we, too, will be "saved" by that message. This is precisely what preoccupies us here: not the "saving" and the not being "written off" of a particular word, concept, or theory, but the question whether and in what sense the meaning of the concept "virtue," and the teaching on virtue formulated in the European intellectual tradition—more concretely, in the four-pronged theory of the cardinal virtues—has a salutary function for our contemporaries. Perhaps more modestly: we could ask what existential relevance all of this has and whether it is important for life—or even necessary for life.

It will be necessary, in what follows, to deal very briefly with two issues in an almost inadmissibly simplified manner. First, it will be necessary to speak of some elements of the concept of virtue; second, the four so-called cardinal virtues, together with the way they are related—in meaning and hierarchy—will need to be described.

But naturally one presupposition must first and foremost be identified and accepted; namely, that man has some obligations, or, in other words, that in his deeds and attitudes not everything is, in detail, right and good. It is meaningless to want to tell a pig that it should act and behave "like a pig." Think of Gottfried Benn's crude line, "The crown of creation: pig, man": that such a thing can be said at all and can in a cruel way be apt shows that man still has to achieve the truly human in his real life, i.e., that, as he exists, he has obligations. Of course, the formulation can be less aggressive than that of Gottfried Benn. For example: "The action of fire is necessarily true and right, but that is not so of man when he does good." That is a proposition found in Anselm of Canterbury's Dialog about Truth [De veritate]. It means two things: on the one hand, that man is free and, on the other hand, that man is meant for something—without prior consultation with him. Precisely this latter element is what all existentialism rejects and which, way beyond the sphere of academic philosophy, influences contemporary man's way of looking at life. This is exactly what is meant by J.-P. Sartre's famous sentence: "There is no human nature"! Anyone who does not acknowledge that man "is" *homo sapiens* in a completely different way from the way in which water=H_2O "is"; that man must *become* what he is (and *eo ipso* is not that already); that we can speak in the indicative about all other beings in the world in simple sentences, but, with regard to man, only in the imperative if we are to speak of what he really is—for a person who does not see or admit this, there is understandably no real point in speaking of obligation and presenting a theory of obligation, whether this be a theory of virtue or anything else of the kind.

There are, indeed, other forms of theory regarding obligation, and a word must first be said about these—precisely to show more clearly what is peculiar to and distinctive of the theory of virtue.

There is, for example, the ethic of reaching perfection by passing through certain levels. It is notable that such theories of progression through stages nearly always presuppose a mystical conception of man—one which has union with God as its aim; with its typical terms like climax, scala, ascent, Jacob's ladder, this kind of ethic is already present in the pre-Christian mystics in the wake of Plato and finds its way almost imperceptibly into Christianity via Boethius and Dionysius the Areopagite. The Christian East, above all, formulated its notion of man's obligation in terms of a theory of stages. The same is true of the early monks and of Byzantine theology. But also in the West there are important names to be mentioned: Bernard of Clairvaux, Hugo of St. Victor, Meister Eckhart, Bonaventura. Furthermore, in the "modern era" the great Spanish mystics, Teresa of Avila and John of the Cross, are influenced in their "systems" by the neo-Platonic distinction of levels formulated paradigmatically by Dionysius the Areopagite: purging, enlightening, union (*purgatio, illuminatio, unio*).

Another, likewise recurring, fundamental formulation of man's obligation is the theory of duties—*De officiis*—well known as the title of a work by Cicero. But the theory of duties found a new and widely influential formulation through Calvin, a formulation and justification which, as a glance at the textbooks shows, transcends by a long way the Calvinist sphere of influence and affects moral teaching right down to our own era. Besides, Calvin provides a biblical foundation for this theory. He quotes from Paul's Letter to Titus (2, 11) (that we are to live in discipline, in justice and piety); and he links the word "discipline" to man's duties towards himself, the word "justice" to duties towards others, and the word "piety" to duties towards God.

Probably the earliest mode of reducing man's obligation to a somewhat systematic formulation is the Ten Commandments; i.e., man's obligations are expressed in a series of authoritative directives which command or forbid a specific action. This the way God Himself speaks in the Sacred Scripture of Christianity—and not only the God of the Old Testament. Even in the New Testament we read: "What must I do to attain eternal life? —If you want eternal life, obey the commandments! —Which ones? —Thou shalt not kill, not commit adultery, not steal, not bear false witness; honor thy father and mother and love thy neighbor as thyself." This is what we read in Ch. 19 of Matthew. A widely accepted type of systematic moral teaching is based, as we know, on the Ten Commandments. It has had particular currency precisely within the Christian Protestant Reformation teaching where it plays an almost exclusive role. This is because of the clearly biblical character of its theory of obligation—whereas the theory of virtue, almost solely followed prior to the Reformation and systematically developed mainly in Scholasticism, has to be seen as something purely philosophical—as "Greek" and therefore heathen.

The thesis about the Greek origin of the theory of virtue is, roughly speaking, correct; but we have to ask whether this is seen as a criticism. For a man like Thomas Aquinas it was clearly not a criticism, although it is not possible to claim him as a representative of "humanism" and its cult of antiquity. "Greek" does not mean for him (any more than it did for the early Fathers of the Church or for Augustine) the same as "un-Christian" or "anti-Christian." Furthermore, it is precisely the element of arrogance and self-righteousness—doubtless often heard in talk about human virtue—which understandably makes the concept of virtue suspect, even for a Christian. Precisely this element is missing from the thought of the great Greeks. For example, Plato's Socrates pensively concludes a long discussion about virtue with the words: "It seems that those who have virtue have it by divine dispensation."

In this context, of course, the historical acquisitions inherited from the past are of no particular consequence. However, a few brief comments should be made. "Greek origin"—that is said too summarily and is not adequate. The doctrine of the four virtues, later to be named the cardinal virtues (prudence, justice, courage, moderation) goes back as far as Pythagoras. But Pythagoras himself is heir to ancient traditions—and not only those of the Greeks.

I have already mentioned Plato. His great pupil Aristotle constructed his Nicomachean Ethics expressly as a theory of virtue (although not as a doctrine of the four fundamental virtues which have become "classical"). This constellation emerges clearly again only with the Stoa; and from there it becomes influential in the Roman West: Cicero cites these in the same order established more than a thousand years later by Thomas Aquinas in a hierarchy of meaning and rank. It seems to me significant that the Jew Philo of Alexandria, long before there was such a thing as Christian theology, tries to show that the doctrine of the four fundamental virtues was biblical, Old Testament wisdom. This was then taken for granted by Clement of Alexandria, but also by Augustine. I will now name here only the most important representatives of tradition—the Roman Gregory the Great, the Syrian John of Damascus, the Anglo-Saxon Alcuin, the Frankish Rabanus Maurus, and finally, Peter Lombard with his Book of Sentences. The reason for this is to show, with a measure of clarity, that in the centuries-long intellectual endeavor, through which one of the greatest discoveries in human self-understanding—the structure of the theory of virtue—has become a basic constituent of the European tradition, all of the forces of the emerging Western world play a part: the Greeks and Romans, Judaism, and Christianity.

If, in what follows, I focus above all on a particular author—Thomas Aquinas—this does not reflect a special historical interest of mine; nor does it mean that a more or less random, personal preference is at work. Instead, it is my conviction that Thomas, through his truly creative selflessness, has been able to weave together into intellectual order the highly differentiated strands of tradition in their contrapuntal variety, without omissions and without resorting to the violence of a system. To achieve this, a completely unusual gift for integration of ideas and a genius's energy in seeking clarification are demanded.

After this rather historical prelude and interlude it is now high time to speak of the concept of "virtue" itself, of some of its elements, and of the four-pronged group of cardinal virtues (asking whether, and on the basis of what it can still be regarded as a valid model—as the model of a comprehensive account of man's "obligations" and of the goals to which he should be educated: i.e., what he is obliged to be and to do).

So what does virtue mean? I am not referring to the word itself (*virtus* is derived from *vir*, man—but this does not take us very far). I am referring to the *concept* of virtue as it was developed by the great theologians. It is a matter of concern to me to speak without using any artificial academic terminology, but I am afraid that making some comments, by way of clarification, about the rather complicated concept *habitus* is unavoidable. Human virtue takes the form of *habitus*, and precisely this is the distinctive character of man. Neither the rightness of things in nature nor the perfection of God can be referred to as *habitus*. So what does *habitus* mean (it is a rather literal translation of the Greek [Aristotelean] word *hexis*)? What is meant, according to the derivation of the word (*habere, echein*) is a particular mode of "having": not the having of something, but of having oneself, self-possession. What man "can" (what he can be and what he can do) is not automatically translated into real being and real action; it is not (as with fire, plant, and animal) that the realization is already included in the ability. Man's ability does not already constitute his virtue. His worth is not based on what he "can" do. Everyone "can" sing, but not everyone is a singer. Only when someone has the *habitus* of singing do we speak of him being a singer. To the bare ability, the free inner inclination and "attitude" must be added the readiness for self-realization; virtue is *habitus*: only by this new taking charge of oneself is man "right."

We have arrived at the point to consider the very brief and precise characterization of virtue provided by Thomas: *virtus est ultimum potentiae*, virtue is the extreme to which our potential to be and to act can be brought. Virtue is the extreme of what a person can be. *Ultimum* means the last, the last in a series. It is therefore something preceded by something else, namely, the "mere" ability given us by nature at birth. This thought contains something important which is not immediately obvious. For the sake of clarification I would like to quote Thomas again, likewise with a statement about the concept "virtue": virtue is the strength through which someone has the complete power which is peculiar to him (*potestatem completam quam habet*) to follow his *impetus*, his drive to develop, his passion for realizing himself.

We are now in a position to know and to name several things implied in the concept of "virtue": not only that man (like reality as a whole) cannot be considered something static but is to be seen as dynamic reality, as being that is happening; and therefore virtue is the strength to follow in freedom this impetus of one's own being, as it is happening, with uninhibited energy. (This makes it clear that to have any understanding of this concept of virtue one must have grasped the completely dynamic notion of man which it presupposes—which is the reason that a theory of virtue of this kind cannot be kept within the confines of a specialist discipline (like ethics); it is not *only* ethics. It concerns man, reality as a whole and its structure; this knowledge cannot be restricted to some kind of isolated morality.) This is not all that here becomes clear and definable. A second element included in this concept of virtue seems to me to be of even greater importance: namely, that man, long before he decides to start out on his journey, is already on his way! Long before he, as one making moral decisions, says "yes" or, of course, "no," he *is* already a yes. Taken in this sense, the concept of virtue means that all human morality has the character of continuation, the development of something long since begun; it is the completion (or more accurately: an attempt at completion) of what man by virtue of *creation* is and "wills"; it can also be said: completion and continuation of what man "by nature" is and brings with him.

I said at the beginning: the fact that man has obligations does not mean that everything he concretely does is automatically right and good. Yet while this remains perfectly true it does not mean that there is no meaningful connection between fact and obligation. Precisely this connection, this closeness to what man, as creature, is and brings with him by virtue of nature and his birth, the link consciously included in the concrete reality of the individual person—this is precisely what constitutes the core of the theory of virtue. Thus Thomas can say: "Virtue puts us in a position to"—in my seminar I usually pause here and ask the testing question: how does the sentence end?—"become master of our natural inclination?" (i.e., that which we are and want, by virtue of our nature and status as creature). That would be quite plausible, but that is not what Thomas says. What he says is: "... to *follow* it"—in the proper way, of course. But there is a big difference between saying one or the other. These are two diametrically opposed positions from which I can evaluate the whole sphere of morality. And morality is not just an aspect of life but the whole of human activity insofar as it is based on freedom and responsibility.

Here a contrasting position arises, against the backdrop of which what is truly meant by the theory of virtue comes clearly into focus. As I said: the theory of virtue also can be misinterpreted and abused—for instance, by suggesting the thought that the goodness in man is like some property he acquires by his own doing, a possession, his achievement and nothing else. *All* theories of obligation have their own particular possibilities for decline. But now we need to speak of the positive, the truly human, the affirmative, the free side of things, which—I am convinced—characterizes the theory of virtue above all other theories of man's obligations (and which could make it, particularly to men of this age, seem plausible and even attractive). To be absolutely clear here, I must be somewhat aggressive and exaggerate a little in my portrayal of the contrasting position. There is, I think, a particular kind of teaching about the commandments and duties, which, while it has no longer much to do with the biblical decalog, nevertheless sees itself as specially Christian and is also seen as such by others. I am referring to the form of moral pronouncing which not only considers as unimportant what man is of himself but emphasizes his nothingness and hopelessness. Quite logically man's obligation is understood then to mean that this worthless being is given commands about what he is to do and not to do from a sphere with which he is totally unrelated—which has nothing to do with his being. The commands bind him in strict obligation. They are commands of an arbitrarily vindictive deity (which is not entirely a free invention of Nietzsche). That is, admittedly, a consciously overstated and extreme position, but it is, as we know, not completely foreign to us. But, in the face of this extremely contrasting position, two things should be clear about the theory of virtue: firstly, how clearly and explicitly man's moral being is focused on—and, indeed, not only the being that he possesses by nature and from birth but also the rectitude which he has to achieve in his actions. Thus Thomas can say, in the prolog to the comprehensive second part of his Summa—therefore about his moral teaching—with completely unquestionable certainty: now we are talking about man: *consideremus ... de homine.* Precisely in Thomas's moral teaching, which may be considered paradigmatic, it emerges clearly that—secondly—man's being is not looked on as mere "material," a prey to an unrelated intervention of arbitrary rules. Instead, man is respected as part of venerable created reality, which, of course according to a plan which no human knowing faculty can penetrate, should flourish and achieve its own proper development—the path to which is opened up and made accessible.

This image of man's developing to his own fulfillment is displayed in the colorful spectrum of the virtues, which are reduced to four: prudence, justice, courage, and moderation. We must now speak of these in an indefensibly quick overview, more aphoristically than systematically.

As I have already said: the order in this series is one of meaning and rank. That is to say, the highest ranking of the four fundamental virtues is prudence. This is an idea which seems remote from us, if it means anything at all. But I have not yet given an exact formulation. Strictly speaking, prudence does not belong in the same series as justice, courage, and moderation. It is not the oldest (or the most beautiful) of four sisters, so to speak. Rather, if we stay with the image for the time being, it is the mother of the other virtues. As Thomas puts it, it is the *genetrix virtutum.* That means, leaving images aside, that justice, courage, and moderation exist only on the basis of prudence! Prudence is the presupposition of all moral goodness. At this point our contemporary use of the word gets in the way—prudence being taken to mean: skill in avoiding the good. ("You think he will stand up for his convictions? Surely he is far too prudent to do that"!) But I will pass over this linguistic aspect. The question is, what is *meant* when the old received wisdom maintains that man, necessarily and always, is both good and prudent—or even: prudent first, and then good on the basis of his being prudent? What is meant is not very far removed from our everyday way of thinking and speaking: namely, the realization of the good presupposes knowledge of reality; someone who does not know the state of affairs is not able, in the concrete, to do what is good. Mere "good intention"—wanting to be just, for example—is not sufficient. "Seeing the way things are" should not be underrated. It is a demanding undertaking, one which is in many ways in jeopardy. In Goethe's words: "In our deeds and actions everything depends on the objects being grasped purely and treated according to their nature." All very fine. But these objects cannot be seen as merely neutral objects which we observe. They are the things which surround and constitute the situation where a decision is required. They are the radically concrete, which continually changes but in which our own interest is very directly involved. What is demanded of us is that we silence this interest of ours. This is a presupposition for us listening and hearing. But everyone knows this, whether in the case of reconstructing events in a traffic accident or of arriving at a correct judgement in the case of a conflict: if one of the parties is not capable of seeing events as they actually happened, the situation is simply hopeless. In this case, the precondition for all that follows is not fulfilled. This precondition—for every moral decision—is that reality is seen and taken into account. Of course, seeing is only one-half of prudence; the other half consists in "translating" the knowledge of reality into decision and action. We could say: prudence is the art of making right and objective decisions— whether this has to do with justice, bravery, or moderation. But, one could ask, is this not asking too much of the average person? There are two answers to this: first, (although it is first and foremost the individual, the responsible and moral person, who is legitimated and required to decide and who cannot be relieved of this responsibility) knowledge of reality is a task which must be tackled in *solidarity*. Each individual depends on others, which is why the ancients consider willingness to learn, to be told something, is an essential element in the virtue of prudence. But naturally this willingness of the individual moral person to be told something—while he still makes his own decision—must not be betrayed. He must not be left in the lurch. In other words, it becomes clear here what the public presence of truth means—also in its negative aspects, namely, in the public obscuring of reality (through journalistic abuse of language and of the media)—not only for society at large but also for the individual making the decision.

The second point in my answer (to the question whether it is too much to ask of the average person to be "prudent") is that to be prudent does not mean to have studied or to be cultured. There is certainly a particular kind of "wisdom" required which can be expected of everyone: namely, a kind of selfless objectivity which is referred to in the play on words which, in the course of centuries, has become a truism in Europe: *Cui sapient omnia prout sunt, hic es vere sapiens*; the person who has the taste for things as they are is truly wise.

If the brevity of this sketch of what is meant by the virtue of prudence borders on the irresponsible, it is almost hopeless to want to say in a few minutes what justice means. We need to start, here again, with the theme of "hierarchy" with regard to the virtues. Of the four virtues, prudence stands alone as the presupposition, the mother of the others which are moral virtues in the narrower sense. I can well understand that the question about which is the highest of all the virtues does not play a particularly exciting role in the thinking of most people. The reality is, however, that this question is constantly being answered (no matter in what way it is formulated). The older generation amongst us can still hear the loudspeakers booming with praise of heroism, commitment, and courage: *this* is the crucial virtue. And everyone knows that a moral system breaking loose from the great tradition has declared itself as the center of ethics. But just as a prominent Thomist, Garrigou-Lagrange, has spoken of the disappearance of the doctrine of prudence in ordinary teaching about morality, it has likewise to a large extent been forgotten that the great teachers of Christendom have given precedence to justice amongst the truly moral virtues. "Men are called good on the basis of their justice"; Cicero had already said that; but the proposition was taken without reserve into the theological systems. Thus the virtue of shared social life was brought into the center of ethical doctrine about obligation—the ability of human beings to live with one another in such a way that each one is given his due. *Justitia est ad alterum.* To be just means to respect the other person and to give him (or allow him to have) his due. Thomas has said it many times: the *bonum hominis*, the really human good, is known and formulated, admittedly, in the act of prudence (we can also say: in the decision of conscience); but it is realized formally in justice, which has the task of creating order in all human dealings. That does not at all mean setting up "society" as an absolute, but it does mean attributing to the social dimension of man incomparable ethical importance. But we are still talking about a virtue, an attitude demanded of the individual and deliverable by him alone. All ethical doings are of fundamental social importance and are therefore subject to the norm: just or unjust. In teaching, for example, I am not concerned with what is true and false or with expressing my own personal opinions. If, in teaching, I just go on talking casually I am being unjust! The whole sphere of the *vita activa* (Thomas also sometimes calls it, in his very characteristic way, *vita civilis*) is defined by "that which is related to the other," i.e., this whole sphere is the sphere of justice, where the virtue of justice makes demands on the individual. The idea that might, as a temptation, sometimes spring to mind in connection with a system of democracy, namely that it could or ought to be possible to create such a well-planned social system that justice would become superfluous (it is an old-fashioned and in a certain sense dubious thing)—this idea has no place in the classical teaching about justice. Furthermore, in the classical teaching we find the conviction that man's world cannot at all be kept in order by justice alone—because, for example, there are debts which, by their very nature, cannot be paid, and for this reason justice has to be substituted (so to speak) by another attitude: of *pietas* (honoring one's mother, for example). I cannot pay back to my mother all I owe her and the moment cannot come where I can say to her: we are quits.

The conception of justice, at all its borders, points into other spheres. This is clear from the fundamental question: if being just means, in all our dealings, being prepared to give to everyone his due, what *is* it that is everyone's due? And: what is the basis for saying that anything at all is someone's due? Can this be decided empirically? Is it enough to have recourse to the "dignity of the person"? Or must we have recourse to an absolute authority? Or: on what basis can power ultimately be legitimized (not just in the strictly "political" sphere, but also in the family, in the school, in business, in the army)? How can power be justified, on what can it be based, when its function is, on the one hand, to safeguard justice, and, on the other hand, is not power at all if it cannot also be abused?

Abuse of power as part of the human condition is a presupposition for the need for courage, which is the third in the series of cardinal virtues and of which we now have to speak. Bert Brecht commented: "When I hear that a ship needs sailors to be heroes, I ask myself is the ship old and rotten." He is completely right. Probably Brecht had no idea that 1500 years before him Augustine said something similar. In his "Civitas Dei" he wrote: "Courage is witness to the existence and power of evil in the world." In other words, because the just and the good do not prevail of themselves, because personal commitment is also required, courage is one of the elements of rectitude for everyone; it is a liberalist illusion to think it is possible to be just without suddenly needing to risk something: one's own direct well-being, the peaceful course of one's day, one's possessions, one's "good name," one's public standing, and, in extreme cases, perhaps even more: freedom, health, one's life. This already clarifies some points. First, for example, that (as Thomas Aquinas put it) "praise of bravery depends on justice" (the order of importance is again consciously marked): i.e., that anyone who fights on the side of injustice cannot be courageous in the true sense; that courage in a criminal is a nonsense. When in 1934 I published my book about courage and prefaced it with the motto "Praise of courage depends on justice" my friends knew exactly what I meant, and less friendly contemporaries knew as well.

Second, I hope it has become clear that bravado, daring, fearlessness, aggressiveness—that all of these are different from the courage which is listed as one of the four cardinal virtues and is part of man's rectitude. Images of risky mountain climbing or dangerous ski jumping *cannot* illustrate (as was attempted recently on television) what is essential to the virtue of courage. In what other way should this virtue be demanded and expected of everyone, including the average man—and therefore all of us?! The act of courage is something completely inconspicuous. To be courageous means: as one who empirically seems the weaker, to oppose injustice and be prepared to incur some disadvantage, whether in terms of condescending treatment in public or being ignored altogether. In the ultimate justification of the courageous person there is normally nothing triumphal. And when there is talk about daring, hardiness, and risk, it is almost a sure sign that the situation is not one where there is real bravery. When these days a pornographic novel is heralded as "daring" there is absolutely no real risk involved. It would be a far greater risk to say publicly that purity is an important part of man's proper being. It would be much more dangerous. The symbol that best represents courage is not the posing "hero" and "victor," but the blood witness. And this witness comes to our attention only *post festum* as blood witness, as martyr. In the final act of being courageous he is put down, ridiculed, abandoned, and, above all, silenced. For this reason the ancients say that the decisive act of courage is not attack, but standing firm in a world which is not structured so as to be in order of its own accord.

But precisely this same fundamental fact that order (not only in the world but also in man himself) does not happen of itself, so that one cannot and may not simply let things take their course—precisely this fact is the presupposition for the fourth cardinal virtue, for *temperantia*, for the virtue of discipline and moderation. This is undoubtedly an uncomfortable presupposition for spontaneous desire. If this desire were of itself in order, there would be no need for controlling our instincts, no need for temperance. Spontaneous impulses are directed to what "tastes" good (in the broadest sense of the word)—what is to one's liking; but not everything that tastes good is nourishing; it is even possible that something that tastes good is harmful, even lethal. That does not, on the other hand, imply that what is good for us will necessarily be unpleasant. The true meaning of *temperantia* can be succinctly formulated: man needs to bring about order in himself. This inner order is not something which automatically exists, as something taken for granted. The same forces which sustain human existence can possibly pervert this inner order to the point of self-destruction. This applies, it seems, precisely to those forces in our being which we would see as those which sustain and fulfill us. For this reason, the preservation of our inner order cannot be a simple arrangement; again and again there has to be a simple, clear "no." How this idea, which is unsettling and difficult to grasp, is to be interpreted is a new question which we cannot address here, but it is evident to an unbiased mind that where the drive for self-fulfillment, for wanting to have, for enjoyment threaten to destroy order within the person, we are required to resist; and that means we are required to practice the virtue of moderation, self-control.

But the truth remains that these forces and drives which are to be controlled are essentially *good*. They are and remain positive. The natural drive for recognition, for example, is not at all bad. But it must, through self-control, be prevented from becoming self-destructive: this comes about through humility. And even anger has its place amongst our fundamental impulses as guarantee of our personal identity; but it, too, must be safeguarded against the destructive perversion of blind, uncontrolled anger. Likewise, the great teachers of Christendom have stated, again and again, that the sex act, naturally, is something good, a value (whereas, for example, in the newest comprehensive biography of such a modern author as James Joyce we read that he always thought of the sex act as something shameful). Chastity, therefore, one of the fundamental forms of moderation and self-control, does not involve the suppression of sexuality but the control and ordering of it.

Naturally I cannot deal with all of the forms of discipline and lack of discipline spoken of in classical teaching about *temperantia*. But I would like, in conclusion, to say a word about one of them — not only because it has become particularly unfamiliar to us, but because it seems to me to be particularly important at this time; and besides, it gives me the chance, arising from the material itself, to sum up in one sentence the conception of man contained in the four cardinal virtues. I am referring to the love of seeing, literally: seeing with our physical eyes. This love of seeing, as the ancients were always aware, belongs to the natural and completely indispensable fundamental impulses of man in his bodily existence. But this impulse can become self-destructive, for which reason it, too, must be controlled. We no longer even have a name for what is being referred to here. The old name for it is curiosity. This is not the relative harmless weakness of the inquisitive lady next door. In his analysis of everyday life Heidegger used the old name (together with this concept he brought some others into vogue: uprootedness, *verbositas*, etc. Unfortunately he just forgot to use inverted commas, since he took all of that from the old doctrine of the "daughters of sloth" [which is the old-fashioned word that was used])—Heidegger, therefore, used the old word "curiosity," giving it its original meaning: namely, the love of seeing for its own sake, the "lust of the eyes," which is not at all concerned with experiencing reality, but rather with possibilities of losing oneself in the world, an illusory world of alluring things deliberately produced perhaps for satisfying this love of seeing. The destructive aspect of this addiction, especially when it has found a tool which is always readily available to satisfy it, is clear to everyone. It is almost embarrassing to name examples; the whole of modern life is characterized by this exaggerated need to see. In this situation, which suddenly turns out to be our own, the controlling of this desire to see becomes a matter of great urgency for us. There is also an enormous pedagogical problem involved in this. The Americans are, here too, already five years ahead of us. They are already saying: education means making people immune to the mass media. All at once it becomes necessary for survival to protect the space of our inner existence, by a kind of asceticism, from the optical and acoustical noise of purely artificial reality—and in this way to preserve or to regain what a meaningful human existence has always been: namely, as far as possible seeing reality—to which God and the world and we ourselves belong—as far as possible for what it is, and living and acting according to this understanding of truth (which is nothing but the manifestation of reality).

This is precisely the aim of the four cardinal virtues: prudence, justice, courage, and moderation. I am convinced not only that this conception can be "saved" (from oblivion) but that it can also "save" man insofar as he meditates and ponders on it, talks about it, and, above all, lives according to it.

What Does Happiness Mean?
Fulfillment in Vision

"Happy is the man who has what he wants." The author of this statement is by no means naïve. He is one of those great writers who
alone, it seems, have the courage and are in a position to make statements of such striking simplicity. It is a statement of Augustine.[123]
In his *opus magnum* on the City of God we can see that he knows
very well the two hundred and eighty-eight views which, according
to the reckoning of the ancient encyclopedist Varro, are to be found[124]
in ancient philosophy on the theme of the "ultimate happiness of
man." This figure would be considerably higher if we included views,
formulated more or less aphoristically, by authors from Boethius
through the French moralists down to Nietzsche and Ernst Bloch.
Also the great masters of medieval Christendom have discussed, in
their comprehensive theological works (*summae*), a considerable
number of the so-to-speak classical designations of happiness—and
found most of them wanting. These days we have little patience for
reading such material. Still, some surprising things emerge which
throw an unexpected light on the subject. And the subject is in this
case nothing less than human nature. For example, one is scarcely
prepared, in the discussion of the all too familiar question about happiness connected with the possession of material goods—wealth—
to be confronted with the concept, already introduced by

123 *On the Trinity* 13.5.
124 *Civitas Dei* 19, 1.

Aristotle,[125] of the artificial, abstract prosperity which, by contrast with "natural" riches, is able to enkindle unlimited desire.[126] A treacherous contrast to the desire for happiness. Or there is the view, perhaps always present down through the ages, that happiness consists in existence itself.[127] This view is the hidden presupposition both for the utilitarian plans of totalitarianism and for the quasi-religious overvaluing of psychotherapy. But also Hegel says: "Happy is he who ... in his existence, enjoys existing."[128] Against such views it must be considered that the quenching of thirst hardly consists in the continued existence of the thirsty person.

And why does happiness not consist in power? I quote the answer given by Thomas Aquinas, who, by the way, does not add any word of clarification to his masterly statement: Power is a beginning, but happiness is linked to the end, the goal[129]—which obviously means that power is something with which the powerful person has to begin something, something which, by its very nature is related to the future and is bound up with history, whereas happiness is always something like stepping outside of time.

All of this, which has always been more or less clearly part of tradition, Augustine had in mind—and much more. He was aware of it and familiar with it when he wrote down his statement, which was meant as defining a concept: "Happy is the man who has what he wants." And, of course, this is anything but an unacceptable simplification. It implies the answer to two extremely difficult questions. The first question is: *What* does man want? The second: What is meant by "have"?

125 *Politics* I, 8f.; see Thomas, *Sum. Theol.* I, II, 2, 1.
126 *Sum. Theol.* I, II, 2,1 ad 3.
127 D. Sternberger, *Figuren der Fabel*. Frankfurt 1950, p. 268.
128 *Sämtliche Werke*. Jubiläums-Ausgabe. Ed. H. Glockner. Vol. II, p. 56.
129 Thomas, *Sum. Theol.* I, II, 2, 4.
130 *Gorgias* 467 b.

First point: what do we really want? The very formulation of this question implies that there is something we only seem to want, or think we want, but don't really want. A certain annoying paradox is unavoidable here, and so I am appealing to a passage from Plato's dialog "Gorgias." In the debate with the young sophist intellectual Polos Socrates maintains that the tyrants admired by Polos do, indeed, what they please but not what they really want. "But are you not saying, Socrates, that they do what they please?" "Yes, I still say that." "And so they are doing what they want!" "No, I say." "Although they are doing what they please? But, Socrates, that is completely absurd."[130] What Socrates is aiming at is to show Polos that, in truth, we only want the good, that which is good for us.

At this point it would be fitting to explain how such quotations from Plato, Aristotle, Augustine, and Thomas are to be understood. To begin with, and above all, they are *not* primarily to be considered for their "historical" importance; our intention is not to find out and present "what others have thought."[131] What I am attempting here is to show that the answers of these great representatives of thought in the Western tradition to the question we are posing are at least worth considering, if not quite simply correct. And I confess I do this to some extent in spite of my own spontaneous convictions.

In the tradition of thought represented by the four names mentioned, the following is said: what we really want is the good—that which is good for us. Even what is objectively bad and evil can only be wanted by us insofar as it appears good to us in some sense or other. —But is this a realistic answer? Quite apart from the question

131 The study of philosophy is not intended for learning "what others have thought but what the truth of things is." Thomas, *Commentary on Aristotle*, About Heaven I, 22.
132 *Man and his future*. Ed. G. Wolstenholme. London 1963, p. 12.

whether we are not able, even formally, to want what is bad, do we not have to say: what people really want is simply to be happy, to have joy? At first sight, this seems quite plausible. Joy is something that we—so it seems—seek for its own sake. Why do you want to enjoy yourself, why do you want to be happy? We don't ask ourselves these questions. And yet this fundamental wish, which requires no further justification, is not as unambiguous as it would first seem to be. Strictly speaking, it does not state that people want, at any cost, to be in a blissful state of enjoyment. What they want is rather that there should be a basis for their joy. This foundation, if there is one, is in truth really wanted; it is prior to joy and is distinct from it. Joy is, by its very nature, secondary. One cannot have joy in an *absolute* way: not for its own sake. The primary thing which is by its nature prior to joy is the foundation for joy—that *about which* one rejoices. One would think that this is completely self-evident, and for the time being I don't want to assume, wrongly, that everyone is of this opinion. But Julian Huxley, a scientist of unquestionable authority, spoke a few years ago of the possibility of producing "an overwhelming sense of happiness" by electrical stimulation of certain parts of the brain; that was already known by scientists for some time, but Huxley added to this (and this is what I think is important): there are people for whom this is somehow too materialistic. He says: "after all, electric happiness is still happiness."[132] I find this idea not so much "materialistic"; it is, leaving aside extreme cases of medical treatment of pain, completely inhuman. Joy which has no foundation, no *ratio*, but only results from a mechanical source, an external cause which can be activated at will—that is an idea which fits perfectly with the *Brave New World* as our brother Aldous Huxley has described it.

But the prior foundation for joy is—according to the ancient thinkers—that one has, whether in hope or in memory, something

133 Thomas, *Sum. contra Gentiles* 3, 26.

good, something that we love and want. In this the two great, yet so different thinkers, Plato and Thomas Aquinas, are of one mind. "Possession of the good is the cause of joy." This sentence from the *Summa contra Gentiles*[133] could almost be a quotation from Plato's *Symposion*—the existence of which Thomas almost certainly did not know.[134] In this thought, that joy and happiness are essentially things that follow as an answer to the acquisition of something good—and possibly a misguided answer but of itself referring back to a prior objective foundation and therefore not a mere illusory play of detached emotions—in this thought something is expressed which transcends by far what is literally contained in the words. I am referring to the confidence in the so-called "real" dimension of life as such—to which belongs the fact, formulated by Augustine, that there is no one who would not prefer to suffer sadness with a healthy mind than to be joyful in madness.[135]

But, as everyone knows, there is no end of things which are "good" for people, which they can want and love, and the acquisition of which can be a reason for joy and happiness. But is "happiness" not too big a word and perhaps even inappropriate if it can be applied to every passing moment of satisfaction in which a person gets something or other that is good—something that he "loves"? The "small instance of happiness" is not happiness as such! The ambiguity of the words has to be considered as well as the tendency towards trivialization and banality. This seems to be true of all human languages—at least for Greek, Latin, and German. For happiness in the ultimate sense—and which cannot be experienced empirically—we like to use a different word: "blissfulness" or "beatitude." One of the terms Ernst Bloch uses, in referring to

134 *Symposion* 205 a.
135 *Civitas Dei* II, 27.
136 E. Bloch, *Das Prinzip Hoffnung*. Frankfurt 1959, p. 122.

what man ultimate hopes to attain, is "*bliss* in a form which has not yet been [experienced]."[136] But the authors of the most recent translation of the New Testament have bowed to the (in my view questionable) work of a team of Germanists, according to whom "blissfulness" is generally a term which can be best used by children, lovers, and drunks.[137]

But precisely the fact that the *one* name "happiness" is used for such different things: the fullness of divine life that conquers death and man's sharing in it; and the tiniest satisfaction of any kind of desire—precisely the use of the same term keeps a fundamental issue before our minds. Thomas Aquinas formulated it as follows: "Just as created good is a likeness of uncreated good, so, too, is the acquisition of a created good a likeness of beatitude."[138] But what is here referred to as "acquisition of created good" occurs every day in innumerable forms: whenever a meal tastes good to a hungry person; when the researcher enjoys a sudden insight; when lovers are together; when a carefully planned project is successful—and so on. But when we call all of these things happiness, and perhaps even bliss, we can still be aware that every instance of satisfaction points to the extreme of satisfaction, and that all experience of happiness has something to do with eternal happiness—even if it only means that in all fulfillment in this life one thing is clear: it is not sufficient to satisfy us entirely. The following words from the diaries[139] of André Gide: "The terrible thing is that one can never be sufficiently drunk" seem to me to apply to every sort of intoxication—and not merely to that of the senses. But the question is: not sufficient for what? And why is it terrible? The answer has to be: because, without any inhibition,

---

137 "Gottesdienst," no. 6, p. 153.
138 Thomas *Quaest. disp. de malo* 5, I ad 5.
139 *Diary 1889–1939*. Stuttgart 1950ff. Vol. 1, p. 105.
140 *Kritik der prakt. Vernunft*. Akademie-Ausgabe. Vol. 5, p. 61.

we demand complete satisfaction of our desire and because in all of this *it does not happen*! At this point the encoded but unmistakable message about the true and ultimate meaning of "happiness" is recalled to mind. The question we began with ("What do we really want?") returns in a much more radical form: what do we fundamentally, ultimately want; what is the nature of the ultimate object of our desire which can completely satisfy our deepest thirst?

This formulation of the question already involves a hidden presupposition which is not immediately obvious and which we probably too seldom consider. The presupposition is that man is by nature needy and, indeed, not only in the Kantian sense as a result of his "belonging to the sense world,"[140] but right through every layer of his being; he is the hungry being as such[141]—which is a rejection of the view of both ancient modern Stoics that it does not befit man, nor is it meaningful, to expect satisfaction from anywhere else, as Seneca famously said: "We call that man happy ... who knows of no good greater than that which he can provide for himself."[142] If this were truly the case, if the thirsty person were himself the drink or already possessed it—why would he be thirsty?

What, then, is in the opinion of the ancients *the* drink which is able to quench man's thirst once and for all? One might expect that the great teachers of Christendom would more or less directly give the answer: God. But that is precisely what they *don't* do. Thomas Aquinas, for example, speaks of the *bonum universale*.[143] The term

---

141 Georg Simmel, *Fragmente und Aufsätze*. München 1923, p. 14.

142 Seneca, *De vita beata*, ch. 4. —Kant is also to be quoted here: "Man's greatest happiness is that he is himself the author of his own happiness, when he feels he is enjoying that which he has himself attained." *Vorlesung über Ethik*. Ed. P Menzer. Berlin 1925, p. 220.

143 *Sum. Theol*. I, II, 2, 8.

is not easy to translate accurately [into German]. The best translation might be "good as a whole"; but it is not meant in any way as something abstract; it does mean something comprehensive but at the same time completely concrete. We could try to define it as something which is so good that in it there is nothing that is not good and outside of it there is nothing that is good. And anything less than the *bonum universale* understood in this sense cannot once and for all satisfy man's desire. It is evident how fully man's utopian demand for happiness, which would seem achievable only in dreams or fairy tales, is here accepted in an almost terrifying absoluteness— contrary to every form of Kierkegaard's "despair of weakness."[144] And naturally the name God can no longer be avoided: "The *bonum universale* is nowhere to be found in the world; it is found in God alone."[145] However, we should not accept that here we are dealing with theology. No, we are simply dealing with a formulation of "finite spirit"—which, although something particular and only a "piece" of reality, is yet, by virtue of its being spirit, designed to be concerned with simply everything there is. But that means that finite spirit—man—is by nature not able to be satisfied unless with God Himself. And this satisfaction by the unlimited good bears in the fullest and exact sense the name of *beatitude*—and all the other names that human language uses for naming the ultimate fulfillment of human desire: eternal life, eternal rest, eternal light, Great Banquet, peace, salvation. But here the words of Thomas Aquinas still need to be remembered—that while everyone thinks of beatitude as a most perfect state of being, no one knows what it intrinsically is, *occultum est*.[146]

Now the second, much more difficult question is to be discussed. If to be happy as such a person needs to have all that he

144 *Die Krankheit zum Tode*. Jena 1938, pp. 44ff.
145 Thomas, *Sum. Theol*. I, II, 2, 8.
146 *Commentary on Sentences* 2 d, 38, I, 2 ad 2.

wants, what does "have" mean? The answer given here in the great tradition of European thought seems (seems!) to contradict all that we are at first inclined to think. But I don't want merely to try to present this answer but to make it plausible. The answer is: the "having" of that which we want as a whole consists in seeing, at least as an act of the knowing faculty; the completely happy person is one who sees.

The challenge implied in this sentence is immediately evident, and, from the point of view of the usual absolute status given to praxis, a definite rejection of this idea can be heard—which is quite understandable. We are not dealing here with something abstract. Ultimately what is being said is: fulfilment of existence comes about in the form of an inner grasping of reality: with all the energy of our being we seek, ultimately, knowledge. The term *visio beatifica*, the vision that results in the bliss in which eternal life consists, is, of course, not unfamiliar to Christians. "Our whole reward is: seeing"—these words of Augustine[147] are quoted again and again in one form or another in the theological tradition.[148] But Plato's Socrates also says much the same thing when, in the *Symposion*, he concludes Diotima's speech about the ascent to perfection with the words: "Only now is a person's life truly worthwhile: when he gazes on the divinely beautiful; this is also the time that he is a beloved of God and transcends death."[149] Statements like these, although both those of Plato and of the Christian teachers primarily and expressly refer to a situation beyond death, should not be taken in a purely eschatological sense. In reality, they also have an anthropological reference. And even the eschatological notion of the *visio beatifica* remains, strictly speaking, if not absolutely incomprehensible, at least removed in our

---

147 *Serm.* 302; Migne, PL 39, 2324.
148 See, for example, Thomas, *Quaest. disp. de veritate* 14, 5 a 5; *Quaest. quodlibet.* 8, 19.
149 *Symposion* 211 d-212 a.

consciousness from any kind of empirical foundation—unless one has experienced that also the concretely existing person possesses in an act of knowledge that which he loves and really wants, and that also for him happiness consists in his sight of the beloved.

That, therefore, is the thesis which is now to be elucidated and, insofar as is possible in matters like this, to be backed up and supported by arguments.

But first a comment recalling that, of the fundamental life forces, precisely sight is again and again extolled in a way which we find astonishing. The words of Anaxagoras, the first Greek philosopher, who taught in Athens a hundred years before Plato, are relatively well known. In answering the question about why he was in the world, he said: *eis theorian*, to see.[150] And in Aristotle's Metaphysics, which must be seen as belonging to the canonical books of world wisdom, we read in the very first lines: "We prefer sight to everything else"—and this is true, as he immediately adds, when we are not at all thinking of action (and, for example, of necessary orientation in the field of praxis). Statements of this kind occur frequently in ancient philosophy, but it is surprising that even a man like Teilhard de Chardin joins in this age-old hymn of praise. It seems a strange and quite inappropriate "Prolog" that he uses at the beginning of his book, The Phenomenon of Man. It bears the heading: "Seeing." He says in the book that in sight all of life is essentially included, *toute la Vie es là* (Vie is written with a capital V!); and: evolution of living things on earth undoubtedly aims at the formation of ever more perfect eyes.[151] A remarkable statement, which contains a complete view of the world!

The main question is: how, and in what sense, can possession of what we love be thought of as some kind of act of knowledge?

150 Diogenes Laertius, *Leben und Meinung berühmter Philosophen*. Ed. Otto Apelt. Leipzig 1921. II, 10, vol. I., p. 66.
151 *Der Mensch im Kosmos*. Munich 1959, p. 3.

The answer begins with a negation. Thomas Aquinas said it almost in passing and without any fuss: in an addition he makes to the words of Augustine with which we began our investigation. It is completely correct (as Thomas more or less says): he who has everything he wants is happy; but (and here comes the addition) attaining this possession and the possessing itself are achieved through something different from wanting.[152] Everyone knows what happens in "acquiring" some concrete thing. I shake a ripe apple from a tree; I take in my hand; I put it in my pocket; I eat it: then I "have" it completely. Fine; the precise question now is this: what corresponds to this grasping with one's hand and the eating of the apple when we are concerned with gaining the *bonum universale*, the "good as a whole," and having it? What kind of appropriation and assimilation takes place? The answer we have already heard and which, at first hearing, sounds repugnant, namely, that this acquisition and possession takes the form of knowing, is not far removed from what people think and know. On the basis of what do I really "have" a work of art, for example, a picture. On the basis of purchasing it? When do I "have" anything from it (a characteristic way of speaking)? One hardly needs to formulate an answer. Of course, I have to contemplate it again and again. I must, so to speak, know it by heart if I am to possess it really as mine. There is an epigrammatically terse dialog, probably of Far-Eastern origin, which expresses this in an ironical short formula: "My garden," said the rich man; his gardener smiled.

If we think about what this fundamentally means, we find ourselves close to traditional thought. The words of Thomas Aquinas[153] no longer seem strange: that knowing is "the finest way of having anything": *nobilissimus modus habendi aliquid*; but, it should be clear, not "the finest way" because it is an intellectual thing (misleading

---

152 *Sum. Theol.* I, II, 3, 4, ad 5.
153 *Commentary on De causis* 18.

"ideal" connotations almost inevitably occur to us here), but because in the world there is no form of having which is more "having" than through knowing. Besides, Thomas is not the only one to say this. While Augustine, who, precisely on this point, is considered to be Thomas's adversary,[154] and whom all voluntarists call on as their great ancestor when they are concerned with seeking legitimacy on the basis of tradition—this same Augustine wrote: "Having is nothing other than knowing."[155] The meaning of knowing is, of course, not primarily the production of concepts and judgements, but *la conquête de l'être* (the conquest of reality).[156]

But is not, with all of this, the significance of desire and love misunderstood and lost? Is not love precisely the way in which we possess what is "good" for us? And since we are speaking of happiness: who is happier than lovers? —I return to Plato's *Symposion* again.[157] "What does he who loves what is good for him really want? —To have it. —And what happens to him who has it? He becomes happy." This is what Diotima asks and that is what Socrates answers. It could not be said more clearly that love has, by its nature, two fundamental acts. One is longing, desire, striving, *motus ad finem*—before the lover has what he loves; and the other act is joy, delight, happiness, *fruitio, delectatio*—after the lover has the beloved.[158] And how does this "having" come about? The old answer precisely to this question is: by knowledge.

---

154 Etienne Gilson also says that, for example, Augustine defends in his theory of beatitude the "primacy of the will" (*Introduction à l'étude de S. Augustin*, Paris 1929, pp. 1–11). Augustine himself writes: "What else does happiness mean if not this: to possess the eternal by knowing it?" *Eighty-three questions* 35, I.

155 *Eighty-three questions* 35, I.

156 P. Rousselot, *L'intellectualisme de Saint Thomas*. Paris 1936, pp. XVIff.

157 *Symposion* 204 e.

158 See Thomas, *Sum. Theol*. I, II,3, 4.

But does one love in order to know? Is that not simply a per-version of the natural order of things, *ein perversus ordo?*[159] This was, early on, the argument used against what was considered to be "intellectualism." But the great teachers of Christendom were not to be disconcerted by such questions—which only need to be formulated a little more concretely for it to be seen that they have no weight and basically no meaning. If knowing really is the finest way of having, and if love is really two fundamental acts: desire and joy—why should desiring to have be better than having, and joy more important than its foundation? And if by knowing God we mean the *visio beatifica*—what is greater, to love God or to see Him? The questions make no sense.

But the objection does lead to closer definition: first, knowing is *not just* knowing. There are levels and grades, which go from fleeting awareness, to rational thinking, to intellectual sight and vision. Of the latter we maintain that it is the most intense kind of possession of what we love that is conceivable. Language does not have any other words at its disposal. We cannot express the presence of something or someone more exactly than when we say: I see it, I see it before my very eyes. —A further definition: sight alone is not what makes for happiness; happy is the person who has what he wants; happy is the person who sees what he *loves*. It is possible even that the ability to see is only fully realized by love—according to the wonderfully concise phrase: *Ubi amor, ibi oculus*, where there is love an eye opens.[160] But it is true in any case that there is no happiness without love. Where there is no spark of affirmation and agreement there could not even be the possibil-ity of happiness—neither in what we see nor in anything else. (Of

---

159 Duns Scotus thought he saw in this phrase a quotation from Anselm of Canterbury. See P. Rousselot, *L'intellectualisme*, p. 48.
160 These words come from *Richard of St. Victor*, Benjamin Minor, cap. 13.

course, no one is unhappy who does not love. Unhappiness consists, ultimately, in *not* having what one longs for in love. Even the pain of the damned is the pain of separation from that which one steadfastly loves by nature.) Love is therefore the presupposition of happiness; but it is not enough. It is the presence of the beloved that makes for happiness; and it is only through vision that the lover experiences the enrapturing presence of the beloved.

A prisoner-of-war report from World War II[161] relates a conversation between two soldiers who, lying on their bunks, ask themselves and one another: what really makes for human happiness? After some to-ing and fro-ing they agree on the answer: happiness means being with those whom one loves. And there is no doubt that for these men "being with" meant above all one thing: *seeing* again.

One of the most beautiful German love poems begins with the line: "When I feel myself deeply contented as I gaze on you" [Wenn ich von Deinem Anschauen tief gestillt ...]. On reading this I am naturally not unaware that lovers do not limit themselves to looking at one another. But it is likewise clear that it is quite possible to "make love" without love, and that, whereas people truly in love radiate their happiness, those who are merely sex-partners give the impression of being frustrated and bad-humored.

A further comment needs to be made here about the biblical language which refers to the union of man and woman as mutual "knowing." The word is not, as one might think, some kind of discreet expression. According to an expert like Martin Buber, the original meaning of the Hebrew word is: direct togetherness, most intimate presence.[162]

If we look for a plausible reason for saying that union with the beloved should be called "knowing," "seeing," it might surprise us

161 H. Gollwitzer, "... *und führen, wohin du nicht willst*." Munich 1952.
162 *Bilder von Gut und Böse.* Köln-Olten 1952, p. 24.

to find that knowing and seeing have, on the basis of their linguistic origin, long since had the meaning of togetherness and presence!

And, of course, this is true not only of the sphere of Eros. It is equally true of the love for children—of which, by the way, Werner Bergengruen says in his posthumous autobiography,[163] somewhat elegiacally, that "it is perhaps the strongest love because it knows that it is not hoping for anything." Everyone knows young parents who cannot see enough of their young offspring and find their happiness [in seeing them].

The happy person, therefore, is one who sees. —The ancients have set up a whole catalog of characteristics which the person who sees and the happy person have in common.[164] It is surprising that this idea has survived in contemporary philosophical discourse about human happiness. Friedrich Nietzsche's[165] posthumously published note is worth mentioning: "The happiness of man is based on the fact that there is for him an unquestionable truth." Truth—that is nothing but the self-revelation of reality which can only be unquestionable for the person who sees it. And the Spanish-American Harvard philosopher George Santayana, in his autobiography, rather unexpectedly gives expression to the same ancient wisdom.[166] He loved walking through the great galleries of the world with a friend who was knowledgeable in art; and when he saw his friend standing completely entranced in front of a masterpiece, then he says, in the middle of his narrative prose, with the obvious claim to formulating a philosophical thesis—"then my

---

163 *Dichtergehäuse*. Zürich/Munich 1960, p. 40.
164 See J. M. Ramirez, *De hominis beatitudine*. Madrid 1942–1947. 3 vols. Vol. 3, pp. 204ff. See also Thomas, *Commentary to Aristotle's Ethics*. 10, II; no. 2103.
165 *Die Unschuld des Werdens*. Kröners Taschenausgabe, vol. 1, p. 84.
166 G. Santayana, *The Middle Span*. New York 1945, p. 142. Deutsch: *Die Spanne meines Lebens*. Hamburg 1950, p. 458.

own burden fell away from me; and I understood that all the efforts of man and of all history to be crowned—if they were to be crowned at all—would be crowned in vision alone."

It would be strange if there were not a whole chorus of voices raised in opposition to this idea of contemplative vision as the ultimate possibility of human happiness. In conclusion, of the many arguments, two particularly important ones are to be singled out for discussion.

The first counter-argument is this: is man not primarily an active being? Is his life not, above all, praxis? Is it not fulfilled by his work in producing what is required for living and sustaining his existence; by his activity as an artist, producing *poiemata* and creating visual shapes? And is man not happy precisely in such activity? The validity of these objections is unquestionable—but also unquestioned. And yet it has to be said that all praxis, by its very nature, is in service to something else which is not praxis. This something is the possession of what we strive for, rest in its possession. Praxis becomes meaningless precisely at the point where it is seen as an end in itself. We can hardly say that the ultimate aim in life is to produce the means of living. —Naturally, it would, furthermore, be contrary to all experience to deny that active life is enjoyable—leaving aside the consideration that seeing is also not simply passive. But it is part of human experience that it is not possible to rest content with this kind of happiness. I quote again the words from André Gide's diaries: "The truth is that as soon as we are no longer tied to the task of earning a living we don't know what we are to do with our lives and that we then blindly waste it."[167] At first sight it would perhaps seem that praxis is here declared to be the only meaningful thing, but in reality here a cool observer is focusing on the deadly void and the infinite boredom which surround the purely practical world like a moonscape. It is

167 Vol. 1, p. 484.

a wasteland which results from the destruction of the *vita contemplativa*. But is artistic creation not a special case, an exception—which, indirectly, may help to make a living but which of itself is concerned solely with the perfection of the work? Is this not clearly praxis yet meaningful in itself? Here I would like to reply with a highly explosive comment, delivered preferably in a Berlin accent, of Gottfried Benn, who liked to underline with particular clarity the praxis nature precisely of poetic production. ("A poem does not come about; a poem is made."[168]) That comment contains an observation and a question; and it is this question, which remains unanswered, that concerns me here. Benn says: "One thing is certain: when something is finished it must be perfect—but what then?"[169] This is not the language of one who believes that the work of art is meaningful in itself. "Then" one would have to be able to celebrate, in the joy of contemplation—of something which is not the work of art itself but which one sees in it and through it.

The second argument against this whole conception of the happiness that lies in vision goes far deeper than the first argument. It can be formulated in the following question: What are we able to "see" when we view the world with untrammeled vision? Is it not full of injustice, hunger, death, oppression, and every form of human wretchedness? How can one look at real human history and at the same time speak of the *vita contemplativa* and of being satisfied by seeing? Is that not a monstrous denial of reality, an unreal idyll, self-deception, escapism?

This argument has several levels of radicality. If the argument means that the world is simply hopeless and absurd and one which I cannot accept, to answer it one would have to go several layers deeper and start discussing a whole new theme—which cannot be done here. Human happiness is only possible on the basis of

168 G. Benn, *Essays, Reden, Vorträge*. Wiesbaden 1959, p. 495.
169 Ibid., p. 576.

acceptance of the world as a whole, and, without this presupposition, seeing, *theoria* in the original sense, contemplation (even earthly contemplation)—which is simply silent perception of that which is—is not to be expected. Such acceptance has hardly anything to do with "optimism"; it can take place also amid tears and in horrendous circumstances.

Although everything that has been said so far does indeed rest on the conviction that the world is ultimately in order and that, despite everything, it is good to exist—*omne ens est bonum* (a conviction which can be shared only by those who see themselves and the world as *creatura*)—the joy in vision, though unsurpassable, is not comfortable because it is a happiness related to pain: not only because the person with vision cannot ignore the disorder in the world and can see in the person immediately before him the face of the God-Man which bears the traces of his ignominious execution, but also because only the "good as a whole," the *bonum universal*, is able ultimately to satisfy us and make us happy.

The expression "not being able to see enough of" which we use to refer to an extreme form of happiness has, if we take it literally, also a negative, painful meaning: namely, that in all the joy of vision we are ultimately not satisfied, and we remain unsatisfied. Konrad Weiß, a German poet who is still relatively unknown, expressed this lack of fulfillment in our desire to see: "Contemplation does not rest until it finds the object of its blindness."[170]

"Manic depressive." The world is such that anyone who knew it intimately would descend into abysmal sadness: even the Word of God, become Man, had to die an awful, ignominious death; at the end of the history of the world evil predominates; Thomas Aquinas says that, corresponding to the gift of knowledge there is beatitude—"blessed are the

---

170 The sentence is in an unpublished fragment in his literary estate: "Über die Armut im Geiste."

sorrowful ...." *Anyone who thinks of this (and it is possible for us to be aware of it without consciously reflecting on it) might well break out into floods of tears and fall into a deep depression—which also might not be "without reason." And on the other hand, reality is at the same time and in no less a real sense so completely—and beyond all comprehension—sustained by God's love, that anyone who thinks about it deeply and knows it profoundly can equally be overcome by an "unfounded" joy which is not motivated by any immediate single cause. This joy can burst through the limits of our understanding.*

And why could a middle position here be "normal"? And how would this normality be regulated?—by the physiological state of the inner-secretory system or the nervous system?

On Music

That the philosopher, especially when he is also preoccupied with matters concerning human development, pays special attention to the essence of music, is not to be explained purely by his random personal interests in music. Indeed, this special attention has a great and long tradition reaching back almost to the beginning of history—to Pythagoras and Plato, and also to the teachers of wisdom in the Far East. —It is not just that amongst the "astonishing things" (with which, according to Aristotle and Thomas Aquinas, the philosopher formally busies himself)—it is not just that amongst the *miranda* of the world music is one of the most remarkable and most mysterious things. It is also not just the fact that someone has been able to say that making music is itself simply a hidden form of philosophizing, an *exercitium metaphysicae occultum* of the soul, which of course does not *realize* that it is philosophizing. (This was Schopenhauer in his profound utterances about the metaphysics of music.) But that which brings music again and again to the attention of the philosopher is its quite special inner significance for human existence; and this is precisely what makes it necessary for everyone involved in education to be concerned with music and music-making.

The question which fascinates anyone philosophizing about the nature of music is: *what* do we really hear when we listen to music? It is undoubtedly something more than and different from the particular sounds produced by the bow on the strings of the violin, or by the air blown into the flute, or by striking keys—even a completely unreceptive person (if there *is* such a person) hears all of these things. But he does not hear what music really is. Then what *is* it that we hear when we listen to music receptively? —The question is easier to answer in regard to the other arts—although the question "What do we really see when we contemplate Dürer's *The Great Piece of Turf?*" is also not easy to answer. It is not grass as we see it—more clearly—in nature or in a photo. It is not the grass, not this "object" which we *really* see when we contemplate a painting in the right way. Or: what do we really become aware of when we hear a poem, when we become aware of the poetic quality of a poem? Undoubtedly, something more and something different from what is *directly* said in the poem (which has even been re- ferred to as the impure element of the poem—of course, a *necessary* impure element). And so these questions are equally difficult to answer. But now the question: *what* does one hear when one listens to music in a musical way? It cannot be a "subject" like ones in the visual arts or in poetry—where *something* is presented, *something* is stated as a subject. In music there can be no question of this, even though this is again and again thought to be the case, even by great musicians. But it is not the "Scene by the Stream" or the "Storm" or the happy gathering of peasants that one *really* hears when one listens to Beethoven's Sixth Symphony. But how is it in the case of "song"? Is it not, at least here, the case that we *really* hear what the text says when an aria or a recitative is sung? Naturally we hear the words. But, in addition to the words, in genuine, great music— when we listen in the right way—we hear at the same time a deeply secret meaning to these words which we don't hear if we listen to the words alone. This deepest meaning is not there to be read like something straightforwardly stated! —And so, *what* do we hear in music? Music "does not speak of things, but only of good and bad." These words of Schopenhauer sum up what has been said in many formulations down through the centuries. It would not be exactly true to say that these words express traditional meaning in an undi- minished way, but they do pave the way and lead us to what is really meant. "Good and bad" (Wohl und Wehe) are related to the will; the good is the *bonum* understood as the essential point about willing. The good is willed. Here we have to be warned against moralistic misunderstandings. What is meant is as follows: the being of man is being in the state of *happening*; man is not simply "there." Man exists as something in a state of *becoming*—not simply as something growing physically, maturing, gradually moving towards death, but—as a spiritual being—man is also constantly in a state of movement; he "becomes" himself; he is on the way. And that towards which he is moving, to which he is on the way (by his very being—it is impossible for him to do otherwise; man is inwardly underway, he has "not yet arrived," whether he is directly aware of it or not, and whether he likes it or not) *the goal to which all this movement strives is the good (even in doing evil the good is intended)*. We can also say (and the great tradition of Western wisdom has said it!): that to which the insatiable inner striving—this fundamental unrest in which the ultimate drive of our developing existence consists—finally tends is beatitude; *before* all conscious desire but also in the inner core of conscious desire we want happiness, bliss: that is the good which is our ultimate goal!

What is really meant by this desire and by the process of development itself in which we—in a thousand apparent or real detours—approach this goal which we have never completely reached: neither the goal nor the journey can be expressed in words. Augustine says: "'Good'—you hear the word and you take a deep breath, you hear it and you sigh." And he says: the innermost meaning and the richness of meaning to be found in the concept "good"—its full realization—cannot be expressed in human words: "It cannot be said, and it cannot be left unsaid ... What are we to do, not speaking and not being silent? Exult! *Jubilate!* Lift up the non-speaking voice emanating from the joy of your heart ...." This "non-speaking voice" (or one of its forms) is: *music!* —Of course, it is not only the voice of *bliss*, but (since the good, the aim of the journey is not easily attainable, since it can be "steep" and the target can be missed!) can also be the non-speaking voice of wretchedness, of hopeful nearing the goal, of longing, sadness, despair. Language is not adequate to express the innermost process of our lived being. The process is prior to language, it is in nature (including that of the spirit) and also transcends it; "that is the reason," says Kierkegaard, "that music both precedes and follows language, showing that it is both first and last." Music makes the sphere of silence accessible; in it the soul emerges "naked," so to speak, without the linguistic garment, "that was caught up in all the thorns" (as Paul Claudel says).

I said that the nature of music has been seen like this, in various forms, in the tradition of Western culture; as a speechless expression of joy and sorrow (Wohl und Wehe) as expression without words of that innermost process of self-realization which we understand as the growth of the moral person, as desire in all its forms, as *love*: this is what Plato meant when he said that "music imitates the stirrings of the soul"; or Aristotle: music is similar to the ethical and is associated with it. There are later utterances like that of Kierkegaard, who says that "music, by its own directness, constantly gives expression to immediate reality"; or Schopenhauer: of all the arts, music alone represents the will itself; or Nietzsche, interpreting Wagner: in music nature resounds, "transformed into love."

This means, therefore, that the inner process of human existence is what finds expression in music (as its material, so to speak), where both have in common that they take place in *time*. But now, since "music" is not an impersonal objective power but is "made" by very individual musicians, also the following is true: that a thousand different forms of such inner processes can emerge as musical constructions and (since the inner development of the moral person is a natural process which is not exempt from waywardness but is threatened in innumerable ways by danger and destruction) a thousand forms can emerge which are false, twisted, and confused. Music can represent shallow self-satisfaction with the easy achievement of the "cheapest" things; the negation of order; despair of the possibility that man's inner development has a goal or that this goal can be reached; it can also be, as in Thomas Mann's *Doctor Faustus*, music of a nihilist, whose stylistic principle is parody and which comes about with "the help of the devil and with hell's fire under the cauldron."

Precisely these possibilities of decadence, the dangers represented by all music-making, have been clear to the ancients, especially Plato and Aristotle, who tried to counter them. For it is not as if the closeness of music to human existence, as the distinctive characteristic of music, merely means transforming into music the fundamental processes of human existence, genuine and otherwise, right or wrong insofar as they concern the relationship of the creative artist to his work. It is not as if there were only great and genuine, shallow and spurious music; and it is not as if—on the other side, on the side of the listener—there is merely a neutral relationship of awareness or non-awareness, of applause, of appreciation or non-appreciation. No, the closeness of music to human existence means much more: it means that, because music directly expresses the immediate reality of the fundamental processes of human existence, the listener is addressed and challenged at this same deep level at which fundamental self-realization is achieved. At this level, far deeper than where judgements are formulated, the same strings resonate, with complete immediacy, which resound in the music heard.

Here it becomes clear why and to what extent music is important for human development—or for the contrary—even prior to any conscious preoccupation with education and teaching. Here we see the necessity of reflecting on these very direct influences— as, for instance, Plato and Aristotle did. It is hard for us to understand why these two great Greek philosophers treated of music so seriously and in such detail in their ethical and even in their *political* writings. According to Plato, music is not only a "means for developing character" but also a tool "for the correct shaping of legal institutions." "It is seen," he says in the "Republic," "as a mere enjoyment and as something which does no harm"; and to think that music is, above all, for the delectation of the listener, whether he has any moral character or not—i.e., whether he is ordered within himself—is a view which Plato, in his late work "Laws," seriously referred to as mendacious. Nowhere can music be changed without serious consequences for the most important laws of the state. According to Plato, that is what a famous Greek musical theorist (Damon) taught, and he (Plato) was convinced that this was true.

Naturally Plato is not referring to the juridical aspect of the constitution but to the actual inner state of the community with regard to its realization of the good. —And so there is very serious, detailed consideration about *which* musical forms, and indeed which instruments should be banned from an ordered society; the Middle Ages also—down to the time of Bach—thought of some instruments as not decent. Detail is not important here; naturally, prevailing conditions of the period are at work. The decisive point is to see (and to *fix*!) the inner link between, on the one hand, the music played and heard by a nation (Volk) and, on the other hand, the inner existence of this nation—just as much today as in the time of Plato!

Of course, we are probably like those for whom, as Plato says, music is seen merely as enjoyable entertainment—whereas, in truth, that mutually conditioning relationship between music— both played and listened to—and the ethos of our inner existence descends all the more readily into pernicious disorder the less we care about genuine order. Our average experience shows, however, that we don't even have a notion that such order is possible, to say nothing of what this order would look like.

If we turn our attention to the empirical reality of life in society and consider how the most trivial mood music, with its cheerful tunes, has become a general public phenomenon—a faithful expression of the banality of cheap self-deception according to which, once in the sphere of inner existence the good has been achieved everything is not so bad and everything is basically "in order"; if we consider what space is claimed by and given over to the rhythms of primitive intoxicating music, music for slaves (as Aristotle said)—where both forms, the music of cheerful tunes and of intoxicating rhythms, find their justification as "entertainment," i.e., as a means to cope with boredom and the emptiness of existence which also, with one element calling on and augmenting the other, have become a general public phenomenon; if we consider that also an incomparably higher formal level of music is sought after and enjoyed as a source of enchantment, of flight from reality, a kind of pseudo-redemption, an ecstasy coming from the outside (as Rilke has said), and that there is music—even great music—that contributes to all of this; if we, finally, consider that parody of creation, the nihilistic music of despair of the great artists exists not only in novels like "Doctor Faustus," so that in all seriousness it can be said that the history of Western music is the "history of the degeneration of the soul"—anyone who, with horror, considers all of these things and has the insight that in music inner existence shows itself (and *must* show itself) in its nakedness, without veil and without distortion, and the same inner existence itself receives from the same music very direct impulses, both destructive and constructive; anyone who sees and considers all of these things will, with a special and new feeling of happiness reflect that also the music of Johann Sebastian Bach, and precisely that music, still exists!

This represents a challenge to us which cannot be met automatically. It depends on our actual hearing of the real aspect of music. This real aspect must, in the immediacy of our souls, be answered by resounding strings—in a newly kindled clarity, fresh-ness, and energy of our inner existence; in the rejection of merely pleasant manifestations of music; in the sober alertness of our vi-sion that does not turn away from the reality of genuine life in favor of premature enjoyment; and in the firmly sustained and unswervingly hopeful turning to the good which satisfies the rest-lessness of our inner desire and which is the real and sole object of the exultation that resounds in Bach's music with its "non-speaking voice."

Music and Silence

Music and silence—these two things, according to C. S. Lewis, are not to be found in hell. Somewhat surprised, one thinks at first: music and quiet—that is a strange link. But then the point becomes more and more clear. Obviously by quietness something is meant which differs from that lack of verbal expression which already in our present existence is a kind of hell. And with regard to music it is not hard to imagine that in hell it is replaced by noise, infernal noise. But then suddenly another aspect of the matter comes to light: namely, that music and silence are indeed related to one another in a unique way. Just as noise shatters both silence and any possibility of communication, together with speaking and hearing (for which reason, in the words of Konrad Weiß, in a time of loudness absolute silence can reign), so, too, music itself, though not without sound, produces a particular kind of quietness—as long as it is more than a form of pure entertainment or intoxicatingly rhythmical noise. It makes a listening silence possible—a listening not only to sound and melody in the way everyone must be quiet to hear something sounding, whether the heartbeat of a patient or a human word, but much more: through music a much greater domain of silence is opened up, in which, all being well, a reality can be perceived which is of a higher order than music.

It is love that sings. (C'est l'amour qui chante.) *In these words of de Maistre something is said about the essence of song, poetry, and music: that all of these derive their impetus from love. This also says something about the nature of love itself: that it can only express itself in song, poetry and music—in the storm and whirlwind of the organ.* (1947)

Silence

Only the person who is silent hears. If someone were to ask me what are the fundamental rules of intellectual life—and spiritual life—I would give him that sentence for his consideration. At first sight, a truism, for it is not possible to speak and at the same time to hear what someone else is saying. But the sentence goes far beyond the purely acoustic. It has more to do with shutting one's mouth; even in normal social intercourse a deeper silence is required if the words of another are really to reach us—and especially if a perhaps completely soundless cry for help from a person who needs us is to reach our hearts. The old saying is relevant here: "To be silent and listen is very hard work." But the idea concerns our very existence. It goes down to a deeper level. All manners of perceiving and grasping reality—seeing, hearing, and any kind of knowing and insight—are relevant. All of these, according to the saying, come about on the presupposition that one is silent—not only, but especially, when one is by oneself in a room and does not have another's spoken word to deal with. The silence required of us in this context is not easy to describe; its opposite, non-silence, has various forms. The openness of one's silent attention can be stifled not only by someone's indifference or by the attitude of a person who knows better and strangles the profound language of things by interrupting, but also by letting into oneself the noise from outside—of the marketplace and the street; the sensation of the day; the optical droning of worthless images which are present everywhere and, as we all know, are at the disposal of anyone who is bored and looking for distraction. The deafness arising from all of that—and it is perhaps desired—blocks all hearing. But the important thing is being able to hear. Silence is possible also with a closed mind, with lips pressed tightly together. And there is also deathly silence. But in reality our silence is not directed at a similarly silent world; things (in our world) are not mute, as one philosopher, in a terrifying formulation, would have it. And the attitude, taught in some Far-Eastern types of meditation, of promoting an empty silence which consciously focuses on no object at all must remain foreign to anyone who sees the world as creation—originating from God's own Word and itself offering the silent listener a message in a thousand voices, the perceiving of which constitutes his true wealth. Goethe, one of the great silent men (which might seem strange to some people), as a thirty-year-old formulated in his diary the maxim of his own inner existence: "The best thing is the deep silence in which I face the world and grow and gain what they cannot take from me even with fire and sword." What one gains in such deep quietness is perhaps precisely the power to speak. Without this listening silence there would only remain unfounded chat, sound, and smoke, if not deception.

Of course, it can also happen that a person who opens himself, down in the depths of his soul, to the truly real becomes speechless, because the abundance of what is now becoming perceptible exceeds the possibilities of verbal expression. For this reason it is not by chance that the "darkness of silence" and "mute exultation" are fundamental terms in the language of the great mystics. And if they nevertheless speak and write about what they have seen and heard, one feels "in the silver of speech the gold of a silence that cannot put into words the secret riches of the soul" (J. Bernhart). Perhaps it is now right, with regard to the most sublime object of human knowledge, for a moment to invert the words used at the beginning: the one who hears is silent.

The horizon of the concept "silence" has astounding dimensions which we experience not only in the wise men's teachings about life. It also has a considerable place in the history of world interpretation. It stretches from the cosmogony of the Hellenistic Gnostics—who saw the unity of the "un-namable" and of "silence" as the world's uncreated foundation in being—to the mystic/ascetic rule of silence of Pythagoras and the monastic orders both of the East and the West, right up to the so charming and profound courtoisie, *with which, in Shakespeare's tragedy* Coriolanus *greets his wife Virgilia: "My gracious silence, hail!"* (1943)

It is one thing to make up your mind not to speak; it is a different thing not to be able to speak because words fail you. Silence of the first kind is strictly human silence, just as word—containing meaning in sounds made by our breath—belongs to the innermost sphere of the truly human. Where the ability to speak is lost, the human being reaches the limits of his existence. This can be a lower limit or an upper limit. Such a loss of the power of speech may be not so much a real silence as a becoming mute.

On a journey through Iceland a friend, my hostess, wrote in my travel diary the Nordic saying: Deepest sorrow and extreme joy traverse the earth without words.

There are physical and mental sufferings that, in equal measure, reduce a person to silence by making him powerless and, so to speak, drive him out of his own nature. Rilke, terminally ill, wrote: "Le chien malade est encore chien, toujours. Nous, à partir d'un certain degré de souffrances insensées, sommes-nous encore nous?" (A sick dog is still always a dog. But we, when we pass beyond a certain level of insane suffering, are we still ourselves?) And the well-known lines in Goethe—do they not mainly invite us to consider: that there is a God who freely gave a man—who had been made mute through his suffering—the gift of speech?

But we lose our speech not only when we are forced down beneath the threshold of our being but also when we are elevated above our ability.

One who, as a mortal being, enters into the light of the divine is blinded, so that just as darkness and the most intense brightness have the same effect on the eye, so also the superabundance of what can be expressed in words becomes inexpressible.

The sphere that is central to human existence, the cultivated field of word and language, borders, left and right, on speechlessness: on the muteness of dumb creatures and on the silence to which the mystic is reduced. But speech drives its roots deep down into the nourishing soil of silence. (1943)

"Sacred" Language

Up to now, finding a useful "scientific" definition of sacred language has not been successful—or so we have recently been told, in a mildly scolding professorial tone. It is worth noting here that, in all probability the definition will never be found. First of all, what branch of science would be competent for the task? German Philology?—not if we are to judge by the minimal success of the recent German translation of the Bible. Secondly, a "definition" cannot at all be expected in this sphere if by "definition" we mean a designation which once and for all puts in words, and reduces to a useful formula, the core of the subject. A definition of this kind also cannot be given for poetic language. That does not have to mean that a sufficiently clear characterization is simply not possible; what it does mean, however, is that such clarification must necessarily be negative and limiting rather than positive. Just as, in poetics, we speak of quality of difference from non-poetic language—the departure from everyday language to the language of poetry which is difficult for an ordinary, untrained sensibility to grasp—so, too, what is peculiar to sacred language cannot be simply defined once and for all for "what it is in itself" but only in the not necessarily constant gap that separates it from average everyday language.

This gap will never seem crucial to someone who is not convinced that there is, in fact, a sphere of existence which possesses the quality of "ontic" reality distinct from ordinary reality. This is already almost a definition of the concept of the *sacrum*—that sphere, therefore, in which (if we are here immediately to express

the ultimate truth) the totally exceptional and absolutely extraor-
dinary event occurs: in the bodily presence of God amongst men.
For someone, on the other hand, for whom this event, which bursts
the boundaries of everything considered "normal," is solidly real,
it is quite obvious, when he is faced with something which is essentially different from the usual, that his behavior and speech will
also be different from the usual. But it is precisely this "difference"
which characterizes "sacred language"! This does not mean some
kind of stilted and pseudo-poetic exalted vocabulary. It is not at
all just a question of vocabulary. It has been suggested, even with
regard to a new formulation of liturgical texts, that one should visit
the marketplace and see how ordinary people talk. But we must
realize that in doing this, no matter how attentively and persever-
ingly, we will never hear words like grace, redemption, salvation,
sacrifice—words which, however, are clearly indispensable for referring to the fundamentals of the Christian faith. But living language is, as we have said, not only vocabulary; it is an extremely
varied web made up of word, sound, syntax, intonation, expression
of feelings and much more; and the different nature of sacred language would need to be such that words of the kind mentioned
(but also much more unusual expressions like "Feast of the
Lamb"!) are integrated into the web without seeming strange or
out of place.

But proof of the necessary otherness of sacred language goes
much deeper. —In the Roman *Instructio* which recommends to the
translator that he conform to the spirit of the different national
languages and to which reference is made in support of some shallow formulations verging on banality—in this same instruction
there are further clearly stated and convincing proofs of the otherness of sacred language. For example, not only is the liturgical
text meant to be spoken in a celebration—which by its very nature
is different from an everyday event—but the real speaker is the
Church itself "speaking to its Lord and making audible the voice

of the Spirit which inspires it." For this reason word is here "not just a vehicle for understanding"; it is, at the same time, "mystery."

How, then, could the speech of the Church speaking to its divine Lord in mysterious celebration be definable, except by being separated from average human speech—not only from its triviality but even from the normality which is constructed by those who are considered to "understand" things.

Preliminary Thoughts about "Celibacy"

If I were to be asked by any ecclesiastical authority whether I thought it was desirable to retain the link of priesthood to the obligation of celibacy, I would not give my opinion. Let that be clearly said from the beginning. It is not my intention to give Church authorities advice. Everyone knows that priesthood and the single state are not intrinsically linked and that there are no cogent arguments for or against the link, but only reasons why the Church considers it meaningful, desirable, and necessary. One would need, to speak here with competence, a deeper and broader basis in experience than that offered by any kind of statistics. And who could claim to have access to such a basis? My comments, at least, are not meant to serve as a "for" or "against" Church practice up to now. They are merely meant to highlight some aspects which I think are neglected in contemporary discussions.

There is, as I have said, no necessary link between priesthood and celibacy. No one says there is. But there is certainly an inner relationship between the two. But this is seen differently, depending on what one considers is the core of the office of priesthood. If the priest is seen essentially or primarily as a preacher or as someone who "reflects on the word," as an organizer of the life of the congregation, as one who "presides" at Church services, it does not seem plausible that he should be celibate. But if, along with the great theologians and the official teachings of the Church, and also of Vatican Council II, one sees in the priest above all someone empowered and called by virtue of Holy Orders to carry out the celebration of the divine mysteries and who, in the person of

Christ, performs the Eucharistic sacrifice for the whole Church, one will see the link between the priestly function and special priestly way of life, including celibacy, as making profound sense and being intrinsically appropriate. Perhaps before discussing the question "celibacy—yes or no?" we should have a clear answer to another question: what is a priest?

It is quite unsettling that amongst priests themselves there is fundamental uncertainty about this point. It comes from all directions. We find it in the answer of the Amsterdam university chaplain who, when asked whether it was difficult for him, after marrying, not being able to say Mass, replied that it was much more important for him to preach. But we find it also in the highly questionable statement of a reputable commentary on the decree about priests in the Second Vatican Council, according to which "the strongest priestly engagement" is in pastoral care and preaching, "whereas administering the sacraments—above all, saying Mass—is, as experience shows, more than anything suffering the ravages of time."

It is also obvious, in fact, that the much proclaimed "self-understanding" of priests is to a large extent at odds with what the Church says about the priesthood. Perhaps this contradiction can be explained on physiological, sociological, and also on theological grounds; and there may be different ways of solving it. As an ordinary Christian, however, I can see no other recourse in this situation than to immunize oneself against impressive private opinions, especially when they claim to be interpreting the New Testament and, for the time being, to be loosely following the teachings as formulated by the Church itself.

If the true and ultimate justification for priestly celibacy is really to be found in the unique relationship (of the priest) to the person of Christ it must, from the outset, seem questionable to make this theme the subject of an "opinion survey" or of a vote taken in the context of Church politics. The explicit refusal to vote, on the part of an astonishingly high number of priests approached, is a marvelous and encouraging sign—to the extent that it is based on this reasoning. The real conviction of the faithful, i.e., of the individual members of the Church, whether priests or lay people, undoubtedly has not only representative but also normative value. But even this conviction cannot, by its very nature, be submitted to statistical research; the persons themselves might not readily be in a position to formulate their conviction or be clearly conscious of it.

In the discussion about celibacy not only does our idea of the nature of the priesthood come into play but also the nature of man as a whole—so that perhaps again we should say: before discussing celibacy we should speak about our idea of man: for example, about sexuality in the whole context of his existence. It would have to be established that, while human beings are man and woman, simple experience as well as anthropological and philosophical reflection make clear that complete realization of the human person is not tied to practice of the sex act. To maintain the opposite would amount to a fundamental misunderstanding not only of the dignity of "virginity" but also of the meaning and the reality of marriage. Introducing the term "virginity"—a word which we feel is not appropriate and which, when applied to a man, seems almost sinister—voices something which, strangely, is hardly ever mentioned in public discussion about celibacy, although priestly celibacy is merely a particular instance of unmarried dedication to God. It is, of course, true that this theme can in no way be the subject of TV discussion or of public panel discussion. That the unmarried state, as the Fathers and Doctors of the Church say, is not be honored for its own sake but insofar as it means dedication to God and—quite apart from all external organization—makes one free for divine things; that celibacy consecrated to God is, through the official interpretation of the praying Church in its liturgy of the consecration of virgins, related to the same mystery from which the dignity of marital union of man and woman derives its ultimate justification—all of this cannot meaningfully be considered and made clear other than in the bosom of the Church itself, in the atmosphere of contemplation which opens itself in faith to the mystery.

We are accustomed when reading of human sacrifice amongst Aztecs, for example, to turn away in horror from such "primitive" aberrations. But it is not to be forgotten that also the death of Christ was, in reality, a human sacrifice, and more than the sacrifice of a human being. *And to grasp fully the essence and meaning of the sacrifice of the Mass it is necessary that, in the consciousness of the faithful, it remains related to this human sacrifice. The un-bloody nature of the sacrifice of the Mass is conditioned not by its character as sacrifice but by the fact that it is the realization of a bloody sacrifice (in bread and wine).*

The Christian altar is, by its intrinsic form, not only a table but also a sacrificial stone. (1943)

"Testimony of Faith"

In theological discussion about the New Testament it is again and again maintained that the gospels are not meant as "historical reports" and are therefore not to be read as such. They are "testimonies of faith" of the first Christian communities. But we have to realize that the opposition set up between "report" and "testimony" is not justifiable and that every thesis based on it is misleading, if not simply false.

Naturally the authors of the gospels are not historians who intended to gather all available material for a kind of biography. But no one can contest—without at the same time ignoring the obvious claims of the New Testament—that they in fact wanted to record and communicate things that actually happened and that were said, even though they made choices and were also convinced, as believers, of the supra-historical significance of what they wrote.

"Testimony of Faith"—this expression can clearly have two meanings. First, it can mean that someone confirms, as an eye-witness, that something happened like this and not otherwise—as a witness who, however, at the same time in faith understands that what he has empirically experienced is a sign of divine intervention. Second, the expression can mean that someone says, possibly in public, what he holds to be divinely guaranteed truth. Wherever a Christian today declares his ultimate convictions, "testimony of faith" comes about in this sense—perhaps, in the extreme case, in the form of martyrdom.

The gospels can only be called "testimony of faith" only in the sense that, on the one hand, the faith of their authors is shown in them but also, on the other hand, that they relate and give witness to something they have directly experienced, something that "we have seen with our eyes and touched with our hands" (1 John 1, I). By being exactly what is usually called an "historical report" they make possible the faith of later generations, although, of course, they do not cause it. Faith means nothing but this: to accept something as true and real on the testimony of someone else who, for his part, is not simply a true believer but who knows the facts at first hand. If there were no one who has seen and knows, there could be no one who legitimately believes. Here, of course, we have to consider a further distinction. No contemporary of Jesus was able simply to "experience" that, in this man, God entered history. "No one has ever seen God; only one person, the divine Son, has told us" (John 1, 18). Precisely these tidings, given to us in human form and speech, are available to us only in the report of those who have written and testified to something they had experienced directly. But if the gospels were nothing more than the presentation of what the first Christian community believed, we would not be justified in basing our faith on them.

"Ready-Made Formal Template"?

I have never yet seen or enjoyed a miraculous healing. But an excellent doctor, a chiropractor, freed me in a few minutes from an extremely troublesome pain which had been wrongly diagnosed as rheumatism and which had bothered me for years. Naturally I have told the story from time to time in intimate circles. If such a report had been recorded on a sound film the audience would have seen and heard a man who, with agony in his face, would have clutched his shoulder and dramatically described the plague with which he had been visited. Then would follow, with scoffing and annoyance, a lengthy litany of frustrations: wrong diagnoses, ineffectual treatment, expensive and useless medicines and, finally, resignation. But then the narrator stands up, folds his hands at the back of his neck, and plays out, as if on the stage and trying to perform both roles, the individual movements with which the doctor releases the cramp: suddenly the pain has disappeared, apparently once and for all. I display my joy and, above all, my astonishment; it has been simply magic. And my friends who have been listening ask me, amazed, the name of the miraculous doctor; one of them straightaway writes down his address. Telling the story of such an occurrence, in this or in a similar way, would seem to anyone the most natural thing in the world. One would not find anything special in the formal structure or in the style of the report—or so one would think. But there is, in fact, a contrary opinion in the textbooks—both orthodox and liberal—which deal with the New Testament with regard to the biblical reports of miraculous healings. These descriptions in the gospels follow, as is to be expected, the same steps and have the same structure as the story I have just told. But that is precisely what makes them suspect. In no way, it is said, is this a sign that something is related which actually happened and was said; it is supposed to prove that the narrators, "the earliest collectors of the Jesus tradition," were influenced by a "fixed schema of a particular stylistic kind, by literary templates and ready-made formal patterns found everywhere in ancient pilgrimage reports"—for example from Epidaurus—as well as in "Rabbinical miracle stories." As a result, we are told how unfortunate the situation is, not just in this case but above all with regard to the "historicity" of the gospels. One of the exegetes most quoted these days intentionally describes that "fixed schema" according to which the New Testament miracle reports were to be constructed; and naturally, what emerges is fairly exactly the "disposition" of the story I told at the beginning: extreme suffering, failed treatment, the healing process (in great detail); finally joy and amazement; the witnesses praise the miracle worker (this latter event is called by its technical name: "choral finale").

But all the learned discourse clearly yields nothing at all which contradicts the historical nature of the biblical reports. One might just as well say that, of course, my chiropractor did not exist either; that the event I described did not happen at all, or, at least, not as I described it, and that the report was obviously constructed according to a pre-existing schema, a model which has been well known since antiquity.

"Post-Resurrection View"?

It is said that the gospels were written from hindsight, from the point of view of the fundamentally changed situation after the Resurrection. After this event, everything that happened previously is supposed to have been described so differently that there could be no longer any question of historical reporting but only of interpretation—of events and of what was said—"in the light of faith in the Resurrection." In response to this frequently heard thesis I would like to offer for consideration an experience which could seriously challenge it and sort it out. During my visit to India an old man approached me in Bombay offering to tell my fortune by reading my palm. In a cheerful mood, I went along with it for fun. He started by putting in my hand a slip of paper rolled into a ball on which, with his back turned to me, he had scribbled something. Then he asked me to say a number between one and nine and then to give the name of a flower. Let us suppose that I could think of at least five English names of flowers. That would give the possibility of five times nine, and so a total of forty-five different answers. And so I named a number and a flower, at which the old man told me to look at what was written on the slip of paper in my hand. Both the number and the name of the flower were written there. He told me quite a lot more which there is no point in relating here. But there was one thing that I was not sure was true. Only two weeks later, when I had long since left Bombay, confirmation came from Germany: yes, it was true. As I had been leaving, the old man said to me: "You will never again set foot in India." I laughed and without hesitation said he was right. I really had no prospect of a second journey to India. This "prophecy" is what concerns me here. It will soon become clear why and in what way.

Having returned from my journey, naturally I told my friends about this strange encounter and this final prophecy. And probably I did not tell it in quite the same way each time; perhaps on one occasion: someone prophesied that I would never return to India; and another time: that my first visit to India would also be my last; or: my path would never lead me to the country of the Ganges again—and so on. All of these formulations, one will admit, would be, if not word for word, quite accurate and true reflections of what was in fact said to me. —And then it happened that in the following year I was, surprisingly, invited to Japan. The flight was via India, with a stopover in Kolkata. Naturally the old man in Bombay came to mind, and I said to myself: either his prophecy will prove to be false or for some reason or other the landing will not take place; perhaps there will be an accident. But none of that came true. Shortly before landing—I could already see beneath me the broad winding band of the Ganges—the stewardess said: we must ask all the transit passengers to remain on board; we are continuing our flight in a few minutes. And only then did I clearly remember that my prophet had in fact said nothing more than that I would never set foot on Indian soil again. And he was completely right. Naturally, from this moment on I was not able to use any of my earlier formulations. I would have had to take them back and even say they were wrong—although "previously" I was completely justified in using them.

Could it not be the same with the hindsight of the witnesses of the Resurrection who heard and saw what Jesus of Nazareth said and did? Were they not intentionally promised that they would be reminded of everything, but only afterwards? And what else, I ask myself, should "inspiration" mean if not the guarantee of the identity between the report and the reality of what happened?

"Jesus, Our Brother"?

When at Mass one hears the term "Jesus, our Brother," or in the Canon of the Mass the Consecration is introduced with the words: "As he was eating with his friends, he took bread ..." one knows immediately that one's spontaneous distrust is justified. But it is worth going into the matter more thoroughly. Naturally one has to begin with the meaning normally attached to such fundamental words as "brother" and "friend," and no theology is needed for this. And to the extent that we have in our ear the familiar "through Christ Our Lord" and, for better or for worse, have to deal with the word "Lord," the problem becomes more difficult; for attributing to this word "Lord" an acceptable meaning is no longer easy for us. Precisely this hesitation finds some support in the great theological tradition, which indeed says that only inaccurately—*per accidens*—can one man be called the lord of other men: that God alone is Lord "by nature." But this is clearly the point which decides the question whether Jesus Christ is our "Brother" and our "Friend"—or "the Lord."

Talk of Jesus as our brother does have support in the Bible. We are told, often enough in a didactic tone, that this is the language of Holy Scripture. But the meaning of the word "brother," as it is used in the New Testament, is not at all unambiguous. Thomas speaks of no less than six different meanings. Not once do we find that Jesus is directly addressed by his disciples as "brother"; nor does Jesus use the term in addressing them. On the contrary he says: amongst yourselves "you are all brothers," but "one person is your master: Christ" (Mt 23, 8ff.) It is something

different when in the Letter to the Hebrews (2, 11) we read:
Christ, as the Sanctifier, did not hesitate to call those who were to
be sanctified by him "brother" because they derive from the common source of holiness—which is why the Old Testament is
quoted; for instance, the Psalm says: "I will announce your name
to my brothers" (Ps 22, 23). It never occurred to the early Fathers
of Christendom to see these words of the Letter to the Hebrews
as an invitation or empowerment for us to refer to Jesus as our
brother. Instead, as Gregory the Great puts it, it was the Lord who
deigned to call by this name the disciples who believed in him.
And Augustine also uses this term *dignatus est* (deigned), meaning
that, out of benevolence, the Son of God as the First Born (*Pri-
mogenitus*) called "brother" all of those who have been born again
into the grace of God—by virtue of his being the First Born,
whereas on the other hand he, as *Unigenitus*, has no brothers. The
Fathers of the Church always speak in their theology, with aston-
ished reverence, of this brotherhood established by Christ, a relationship which *He* has the right to call such but we do not.
Clement of Alexandria, trained in philosophy and literature,
strangely thought it necessary to make this notion plausible to his
readers by using a quotation from Homer's *Iliad* (4, 155). He says
that only the martyr, on the basis of his dying as witness, can come
"to the Lord as to a friend" and may then hear from the lips of his
Savior "the greeting 'dear brother'—to use these words of the
poet."

Now with regard to "the meal He shared with His friends" on
the eve of his suffering and death, this is, first of all, not primarily
a social gathering but a sacrificial meal, a sacred ritual; and, secondly, it is not friends with whom Jesus celebrates, but, as He himself called them (Lk 6, 13), his "Apostles." An apostle, however, is
something different from a friend; apostles are sent, and indeed,
as Jesus himself says, "like lambs to the wolves" (Lk 10, 3). He certainly called the twelve his friends, "no longer servants, but

friends"; but he adds immediately, in the same breath, a warning against any misunderstandings: "You have not chosen me, but I have chosen you" (John 15, 15f.). Here Thomas Aquinas raises the point in his Commentary on the Gospel of John: "Amongst men it is consistently the case that each sees in himself the basis for friendship: 'each friend says: I, too, have formed a friendship' (Sir 37, 1). But to exclude this possibility, the Lord adds: you have not chosen me—as if saying: anyone called to the dignity of this friendship should not see the foundation for it in himself but in me, since I choose him for it. 'It is not you who have chosen me as your friend, but it is I who have chosen you', i.e., I make friends of you."

Because, therefore, Jesus can make us and call us his brothers and friends whereas we cannot make Him our brother and friend as if there existed a simple reciprocity; because, on the contrary it is true that "you call me master and Lord, and you are right: I am master and Lord" (John 13, 13)—to which Chrysostomos comments that, while Jesus accepts the judgement of his disciples, he, however, makes it clear that this judgement is true not because it reflects the opinion of his disciples: for this reason, starting with Peter's Pentecost speech (Acts 2, 36), and since the earliest letters of Paul up to the prayers of the liturgy following the Second Vatican Council—the Church, speaking as such, has never named and addressed Jesus Christ other than with the name *Kyrios*, "Lord." Less correct names expressing a particular aspect may come into the foreground again and again, but they will never dislodge the name which expresses the core reality—whether the other names be: brother, friend, the man for other people, man of God, man of the Lord. This latter designation, *homo dominicus*, was for a time seen even by Augustine as meaningful and feasible when he was under the influence of fashionable (Apollinarian) thinking. But in the late self-critical book of *Retractationes* he rejects this term: "I wish I had never said it"; and: "I do not see how Jesus Christ can justifiably be called 'man of the Lord'; he is 'the Lord' pure and simple."

Bibliographical Notes

Individual essays were already published in the volume "Weistum, Dichtung, Sakrament" (Kösel-Verlag, Munich 1954), which is now out of print. Such essays are marked below with (W) for identification.

What does Interpretation mean?—a greatly abbreviated version of a lecture given in September 1978 at the Rhine-Westphalia Akademie der Wissenschaften in Düsseldorf. It was published in its entirety, together with the discussion that followed, in the Westdeutschen Verlag, Opladen 1979.

Theology and Pseudo-Theology—printed with the title "Buchstabier-Übung" in the Internationale Katholischen Zeitschrift "Communio" (3, 1974). The same applies to the two following essays:
The Faith of Socrates (3, 1974)
Two Ways of Being "Critical" (4, 1975)

Createdness—published in the collection of essays edited by Ludger Oeing-Hanfoff: "Thomas von Aquin 1274/1974," Kösel-Verlag, Munich 1974. Delivered as a lecture in abbreviated form at the Internationer Thomas-Kongresss (Rome-Naples, April 1974) under the title "The Concept of Createdness and Its Implications"; printed in the first volume of the Kongress-Akten (Rome 1974).

Sartre's Proof for God's Existence—published under the title "Buchstabier-Übung" in the "Internationale Katholische Zeitschrift 'Communio'" (4, 1975).

The Blind Spot (W)
Agendo patimur esse (W)

Sign and Symbol as Language of the Christian Faith—lecture held at a Church Building conference in Mainz (25 April 1979) organized by the Artists Union, Cologne.

Thought has its beginnings ... (W)

Gifts of the Greeks... (W)

Knowledge and Freedom (W)—a lecture held in the Hamburg Town Hall at the opening of the International Congress "Wissenschaft und Freiheit," organized by the University of Hamburg and the "Kongress für die Freiheit der Kultur." The text is slightly abbreviated.

Freedom and Pornography—published under the title "Buchstabier-Übung" in the "Internationale Katholische Zeitschrift 'Communio'" (4, 1975).

Philosophy and the Common Weal (W)—originally published under [this English title] in the Harvard journal "Confluence" (Vol. 1, 1952), edited by Henry Kissinger.

The Intrinsic Split in All Earthly Rule (W)

Contemporary Relevance of the Cardinal Virtues—lecture held at a colloquium of the Lindenthal-Institute in Cologne (June 1974); printed in "Altes Ethos—Neues Tabu," Adamas Verlag, Cologne 1974.

What Does Happiness Mean? Contribution to a lecture series organized by the Carl-Friedrich-von-Siemens-Stiftung in Munich;

printed, along with the other lectures (including those by Friedrich Georg Jünger, Arnold Gehlen, Viktor E. Frankl) in "Was ist Glück?" (Deutscher Taschenbuch-Verlag, Munich 1976).

"Manic Depressive" (W).

On Music (W)—a speech at a Bach Concert in the Pädagogischen Akademie Essen (Winter 1951/52).

Music and Silence—published as "Buchstabier-Übung" in the "Internationale Katholische Zeitschrift 'Communio'" (4, 1975).

C'est l'amour qui chante (W).

Silence—published in a meditation series edited by the "Informationszentrum Berufe der Kirche" (Freiburg i. Breisgau).

Horizon of the Concept of "Silence" (W).

"It is one thing, by one's own deliberate act..." (W)

"Sacred" Language—appeared as "Buchstabier-Übung" in the "Internationale Katholische Zeitschrift 'Communio'" (4, 1975).

On the theme of Celibacy: An essay requested by the "Katholische Nachrichten Agentur" (KNA), and published by, amongst others, the Berlin "Petrusblatt" (1969, no. 25).

The Altar: Table and Sacrificial Stone (W)

Testimony of Faith?—appeared as "Buchstabier-Übung" in the "Internationale Katholische Zeitschrift 'Communio'" (3, 1974). The same applies to:

Ready-made Formal Templates? (3, 1974) and
"Post-Resurrection" View? (3, 1974) and
"Jesus, our Brother"? (4, 1975).

Index

Index

This title, which at first sight seems curious, shows Pieper's philosophical work as rooted in the basics. He takes his inspiration from Plato – and his Socrates – and Thomas Aquinas. With them, he is interested in philosophy as pure theory, the theoretical being precisely the non-practical. The philosophizer wants to know what all existence is fundamentally about, what "reality" "really" means. With Plato, Pieper eschews the use of language to convince an audience of anything which is not the truth. If Plato was opposed to the sophists – among them the politicians – Pieper is likewise opposed to discourse that leads to the "use" of philosophy to bolster a totalitarian regime or any political or economic system.

A fundamental issue for Pieper is "createdness." He sees this as the fundamental truth of our being – *all* being – and the fundamental virtue we can practice is the striving to live according to our perception of real truth in any given situation. The strength and attraction of Pieper's writing is its direct and intuitive character which is independent of abstract systematization. He advocates staying in touch with the "real" as we experience it deep within ourselves. Openness to the totality of being – in no matter what context being reveals itself – and the affirmation of all that is founded in this totality are central pillars of all his thinking. Given the "simplicity" of this stance, it is no surprise that much of it is communicated – and successfully – through his gift for illustration by anecdote. Like Plato, this philosopher is a story-teller and, like him, very readable.

ST. AUGUSTINE'S PRESS
South Bend, Indiana
www.staugustine.net

ISBN 978-1-58731-232-8

US$18.00

9 781587 312328